JAPAN

A HANDBOOK IN INTERCULTURAL COMMUNICATION

Tomoko Koyama

National Centre for English Language Teaching and Research
Macquarie University, Sydney NSW 2109

Japan: A Handbook in Intercultural Communication

Published and distributed by the
National Centre for English Language
Teaching and Research
Macquarie University
Sydney NSW 2109

ISBN 0 85837 734 9
ISSN 1036 1030

© Macquarie University 1992

Copyright
The law allows the reader to make a single copy
of part of a book for purposes of private study. It
does not allow the copying of entire books or the
making of multiple copies of extracts. Written
permission for any such copying must always be
obtained from the publisher in advance.

Typeset by Photoset Computer Service, Sydney NSW 2000
Printed by Clarendon Printing Pty Ltd, Lewisham NSW 2049
Cover Design by Simon Leong Design

TABLE OF CONTENTS

	Page
Preface	
CHAPTER 1	
Introduction	1
What is Cross-Cultural Communication?	1
Language and Culture	2
Culture and Language Teaching	3
Teaching Culture	4
About This Book	4
A Word of Warning	5
Cross-Cultural Communication and Culture Shock	5
CHAPTER 2	
Background: The Land and the People	9
Geography	9
Population	10
History	10
Government	16
Religion	17
CHAPTER 3	
Features of the Japanese Language	19
The Japanese Sound System	19
The Japanese Writing System	22
Japanese Grammar	26
Japanese Honorifics	33
Chapter 4	
Defining Self in Society	39
Names	39
Addresses	40
Date of Birth	40
Age	41
Occupation	41
Ethnicity	42
Terms of Address	45
Family Relationships	49
Friendship	53
Leisure Activities	55
Meeting People and Making Casual Conversation	57
Male/Female Relationships	60
Chapter 5	
Living in Society	63
Employment	63

TABLE OF CONTENTS *(continued)*

	Page
Housing	70
Banking	75
Service Encounters	75
Health	79
Getting Around	81

Chapter 6
Interacting in Society — **83**

Greetings	83
Introductions	85
Leave-taking	86
Agreeing, Disagreeing and Expressing Opinions	89
Complimenting	91
Asking for Permission	93
Offering, Declining and Accepting	95
Apologising	97
Thanking	99
Complaining	101
Requesting Assistance	102
Asking for Information	103
Expressing Ability	104
Expressing Emotions	105
Aizuchi or 'back-channelling'	106
Do you mean 'yes' or 'no'?	108
Some General Considerations on Japanese Interaction Patterns	109

Chapter 7
Values — Thinking in Society — **111**

The Concept of the Individual	111
The Role of the State	112
The Concept of Harmony: *Wa*	112
The Importance of Reciprocity	113
The Importance of Education	114
The Importance of Age	115
The Concepts of *Uchi* and *Soto*	115

Chapter 8
The Japanese Student in the Classroom — **121**

English Education in Japan	121
Attitudes to Learning	122
The Roles of Teacher and Student	122
The Education System	123

Chapter 9
Recommended Reading — **129**

ACKNOWLEDGEMENTS

I would like to thank the staff of the Japanese Studies section of the School of Modern Languages at Macquarie University, and in particular Christine Dudley who has given me great support and encouragement. Special thanks are also due to Jean Brick, Professor Chris Candlin and Collin Noble for their guidance and helpful comments. Helen Lucey gave invaluable last minute help in proofreading the manuscript. Finally, without the enthusiasm and encouragement of Sue Benson, Liz Goodman and Jennie Skinner of the Resources and Publications Section of the National Centre for English Language Teaching and Research, this book would not have appeared.

PREFACE

Japan: A Handbook in Intercultural Communication is the second in the series *Language and Culture* produced by the National Centre for English Language Teaching and Research. The series is based on the assumption that language is one of the cornerstones of a culture, reflecting its values, attitudes and behaviour; and that language both determines and is determined by such values, attitudes and behaviour. It is therefore impossible to teach or learn a language without also teaching or learning something at least of the culture that it expresses.

During the last twenty years, language teaching has been transformed by what might be called the communicative revolution. Building on the work of Hymes (1972) and Halliday (1985) in particular, the increasing interest in communicative approaches to language teaching has focused attention on how the social setting of language and the roles adopted by participants in an interaction influence the language used in communication.

Participant roles and relationships, social setting and other features of what Halliday calls the context of situation are seen as determinants of what can be said, to whom, where and when. Participants in an interaction use their knowledge of such roles and relationships both to formulate their own utterances and to interpret the utterances of others.

Communicative language teaching reflects these findings in many ways: language is presented to learners in carefully defined contexts, attention is devoted to establishing the relationship between participants, students are asked to perform tasks that necessitate the active use of the language in contexts designed to imitate as far as possible real-life situations.

However important these changes may have been, they fail in two significant respects. While acknowledging the importance of role relationships and of context in determining communication, theory has tended to ignore the wider context, at least as far as communicative language teaching goes. The matrix of attitudes, values and beliefs that themselves are crucial in determining what is regarded as appropriate in specific social roles and specific situations, has not been given due attention.

Related to this failure is the general assumption (an unanalysed assumption shared by syllabus and materials writers as well as by classroom teachers) that attitudes, values and beliefs are in many ways shared across cultures. Baldly stated like this, the vast majority of educators would immediately protest. However, the most cursory examination of teaching texts will tend to support the claim. There are units on apologising, on greeting and leave-taking, on talking about past events, but these are presented as if the content remains constant across cultures while the language used to express them changes. We ask our students, 'Did you have a good weekend' and assume their hesitant replies are due to difficulties with the language rather than the content of the question. Little attention is devoted to examining Australian assumptions about egalitarianism, for example, that are realised in so many of the interactions that characterise Australian daily life. Even less attention is given to examining the assumptions that language learners bring to interpreting and framing their interactions, assumptions that inevitably influence their use of English.

The *Language and Culture* series represents an initial step towards integrating consideration of attitudes, values and behaviours into the process of language teaching. This integration needs to take place at every level of language teaching and learning, from needs analysis and curriculum planning to materials design and classroom methodology. At the needs analysis level, we need to consider students' assumptions about effective ways of learning. In planning curriculum, we need to identify the values, attitudes and assumptions that are realised in the language to be taught and to develop materials that will allow these to be explored. This means giving both students and teachers the opportunity to investigate the values, attitudes and assumptions realised both in L1 and in L2.

It is obviously not possible to describe any particular culture completely, nor all the attitudes, values and behaviour patterns of that culture. However, just as within the grammatical system of a language, for teaching purposes, we make choices about areas to describe in greater or lesser detail, so, in relation to culture, we can describe relevant sub-systems. This series is concerned with the exploration of some of the sub-systems relevant to different cultural groups.

The great danger in any approach that involves generalisations about attitudes and values is the danger of stereotyping. Stereotyping tends to arise when predictions about the behaviour of an individual or a group of individuals are made on the basis of preconceived ideas about the attitudes and behaviour patterns of that individual or those individuals. However, a culture is made up of many interlocking sub-systems of values, attitudes and behaviours, each of which is not a clearly defined concept but a fuzzy continuum. At the same time, various sub-systems are not necessarily compatible. Like the Red Queen, we are all capable of believing several contradictory things before breakfast. Nor are attitudes (or cultures) stable or fixed; they are subject to modification in response to a myriad external and internal stimuli — modification that occurs, moreover, at both group and individual level. All this means that it is impossible to predict how anyone will react under certain conditions. Which particular aspects of his or her culture an individual will call on in any given situation is that person's decision, determined by the interaction of the many assumptions prevailing at the time.

The aim of this series then is not to facilitate the prediction of individual behaviour. It is rather to help in the interpretation of behaviour. The series aims to assist learners to interpret the language and behaviour of Australians in ways that Australians themselves would consider correct. At the same time, it aims to help teachers accurately interpret the behaviour of their students. The focus is on the development of the skills necessary to correctly interpret unfamiliar behaviour, and to participate with confidence in situations commonly encountered in daily life.

Throughout the series, the term 'Australian' has been used to refer to someone who, regardless of ethnic background or place of birth, has acquired the social behaviour, values and beliefs recognised by the majority of Australian residents as 'Australian.' These behaviours, values and beliefs have an Anglo-Celtic base but have been modified by Australians according to local conditions and as a result of interaction with other ethnic immigrant groups.

Some topics are touched upon more than once because they are examined from different points of view. For example, age is discussed in Chapter 4 in the context of how Japanese identify themselves, and again in Chapter 7 where Japanese value systems are considered.

This book examines the attitudes and values, the beliefs and behaviour patterns that Japanese learners of English are likely to bring to the task of language learning. It represents a significant contribution to the task of helping Australian teachers understand their Japanese students and, conversely, assists Japanese students in gaining a deeper appreciation of Australians and their culture.

Jean Brick
Series Editor

CHAPTER ▪ ONE

INTRODUCTION

What Is Cross-Cultural Communication?

Several years ago, two Australian university students went to Japan to study Japanese language and culture. They had majored in Japanese studies for three years in Australia and so a year in Japan was like a dream come true.

One of these students was interested in Japanese art. She enrolled in pottery and ink-painting classes and enjoyed visiting museums and temples to see the artworks she had learned about in university. The other spent most of her time mixing with Japanese people. Through youth committees and volunteer groups she tried as much as possible to integrate into Japanese society. By establishing this kind of close contact with many people she gradually learned how Japanese society worked and the ways in which Japanese interacted with each other.

On their return to Australia, both students commented on how much their cultural understanding of Japan had increased. Certainly, their understanding of Japanese culture had been enhanced, but they seemed to have approached Japanese culture from completely different perspectives. What is this difference in describing culture? And what exactly do we mean when we say 'culture'?

Members of a culture share certain things in common. History, customs, art, music — these are all elements of 'culture'. *Waltzing Matilda*, for example, conveys a message which reflects certain aspects of the Australian identity. Australia Day — simply another day for people in other countries — carries a special significance for Australians.

In a narrow sense, culture is an observable entity consisting of tangible elements such as art and music. However, there are other aspects of culture which are closely related to patterns of communications.

Members of the same culture share scenarios or models that determine the speech and behaviour appropriate to a given situation. Such scenarios, which include commonly accepted values and attitudes, determine the range of roles that individuals can assume and are reflected in the ones they choose to adopt. Successful communication depends upon the participants — whatever the form of interaction taking place — sharing common assumptions on the likely interpretation of their behaviour. Such behaviour is largely — though by no means exclusively — linguistic.

Participants in a conversation are therefore expected to interpret mainly linguistic signals in order to achieve successful communication. In an Australian context, for example, people interpret 'How are you?' as a greeting to be answered with a similar short phrase. People do not expect to stand in front of a lift for an hour discussing the full details of their health. 'How are you?' is a signal that allows Australians to acknowledge each other. Similarly, when neighbours on the street in Japan ask 'Where are you going?', the question is treated as a greeting, not as a request for information.

Scenarios are crucial in interpreting what is going on in a given situation and what reactions are expected. They allow an individual to interpret how the world works. Scenarios vary from culture to culture, so that a person entering a new culture needs to acquire some knowledge of its scenarios. It is, of course, true that scenarios are not absolute; that is, they do not dictate the behaviour of every individual under all circumstances. Communication is a dynamic activity in which the participants themselves decide what meaning they want to convey in any particular interaction. However, if the participants do not share common scenarios that allow them to interpret others' behaviour, then communication is likely to be ineffective. Awareness of communication patterns is the key to successful cross-cultural communication. It is therefore essential to describe and explain the scenarios that underlie communication patterns.

Language and Culture

'I will give it positive consideration'. This typical phrase, used in Japanese to indicate a negative answer, often causes great misunderstanding. In business, the phrase pleases the Australian businessman in the short term because it is interpreted as an indication that negotiations are promising. A Japanese businessman, however, uses it to refuse in an indirect manner so as not to cause offence.

This kind of misunderstanding is very common, as people often read the signals of someone from another culture by drawing on their own cultural framework. In the above example, the Japanese businessman tried to avoid confrontation while the Australian expected issues to be treated openly. Avoidance of confrontation among Japanese and directness among Australians reflect social values which, when manifested in communication, invite misunderstanding.

The Japanese act of 'refusal' is often carried out by implication, while among Australians refusal is more frequently openly stated and accompanied by appropriate explanations.

As the above example indicates, language reflects the values and the beliefs shared by members of a common culture. Interactions involving people from different cultural backgrounds require an understanding and appreciation of the culture which influences the language.

Culture and Language Teaching

Very few teachers would disagree that language teaching means more than just the teaching of grammar and vocabulary. Conscientious language teachers are aware that a language is a reflection of its culture. Language and cultural values are interwoven in patterns of communication.

In the classroom, teachers simulate various situations and it is assumed that students will put into practice the language they learn in these artificial situations when they are communicating in the outside world. In reality, however, many students find it uncomfortable to actually use what they have learnt. Many Japanese students of English, for example, feel it rather arrogant to assert their own opinions. One student expressed it like this: 'I felt that I was being very selfish when I said "I don't think so." I was not comfortable about expressing opposing ideas. I felt as if I was having a fight with that person.'

While Australians generally expect to reach a solution by exchanging conflicting or at least contrasting points of view, Japanese students tend to interpret such behaviour as arrogance. They may feel confused in their English classes because they do not understand why they are learning how to express disagreement. They are caught between the patterns of communication appropriate in English and the patterns of their native Japanese. Consequently, they may become passive and withdraw from active participation in everyday communication in English.

Classroom activities tend to become rather one-sided. That is, they may concentrate on 'this is how we do things' and ignore the students' own cultural rules. As a result, while teachers strive to make classroom tasks practical and closely related to everyday situations, students are often not confident about using what they have been taught. Within the classroom they are able to participate in activities, thanks to the teacher's guidance and their familiarity with their classmates, but when placed in an actual situation without anyone to help them, they tend to feel disorientated.

In order to successfully acquire communication skills, students need to learn not only what native speakers would say in a certain situation, but also why they would act in that way.

Teaching Culture

The purpose of this book is to help language teachers integrate aspects of cultural considerations into the process of language teaching. Its basic premise is that both teachers and students need to explore cultural issues.

The aim of integrating culture into language teaching is not, however, to teach culture. Such an attempt would be impossible and even presumptuous. The main object of the exercise is for teachers and students equally to become aware that different languages express different cultural meanings. This needs to be done by means of mutual exploration. Australian teachers, for example, expect their students to call them by their first name, while students from many other cultural backgrounds may find this custom uncomfortable. In Japan, teachers are looked up to and therefore should be addressed as 'Teacher' or as 'Teacher Smith'. By addressing their teachers by their first name, some students may feel that they are violating the behaviour required of a person in the role of a 'student' and undermining the respect due to someone in the role of a 'teacher'. Some may take the informality of Australian terms of address as indicating that Australian teachers are primarily friends. Teachers too may misunderstand their students. It is common to hear them commenting among themselves along the following lines: 'Japanese students are so hard to understand. They are so lively and chatty among themselves, but suddenly become meek as lambs in the classroom.'

As with terms of address, different cultures attach different meanings to similar behaviours. The consequences are misunderstanding and even distrust.

Through mutual discovery in the classroom, the major skills necessary for successful cross-cultural communication can be developed — the ability to suspend judgment, to analyse situations as a native speaker would analyse them and to decide on courses of action appropriate to the situation. In other words, both students and teachers need to learn to explore the cultural logic expressed in what is said and done in any given situation.

Ultimately, awareness of why certain things are done in certain situations under certain circumstances enhances the understanding of the world view and values of both cultures. Students are then equipped to respond to individual and unique situations in an appropriate manner.

About This Book

This book is designed to create opportunities for cross-cultural learning. Firstly, it presents concise information for teachers regarding aspects of Japanese history, geography and language. It then discusses Japanese values and beliefs with specific reference to common linguistic functions such as expressing agreement and disagreement, asking for and giving information and offering, accepting and declining. The values and behaviour patterns explored and the aspects of everyday life presented have been chosen with reference to the linguistic functions and the situations found in most general English language courses. The aim is to facilitate comparison and contrast of the values, behaviour and language appropriate to similar situations in the cultures of Japan and Australia.

I have used case studies extensively to illustrate the situations under discussion and have also provided information about how Japanese tend to view Australian attitudes and values.

The tasks provided aim to involve every member of the class in reflecting on cultural issues. Students are invited to report on what they would do or how they would react in given situations and to compare their reactions to those of the teacher. They are expected to analyse situations for themselves and then exchange results and opinions with other students and with the teacher, analysing differences and similarities in the chosen courses of action.

The aim of the tasks is to train students to analyse situations independently and to enhance their learning skills. At the same time, teachers are encouraged to analyse both their own culture and the culture of their students.

A Word of Warning

In the analysis of cultural issues, it must be remembered that there is no such thing as an absolute representation. Cultural rules are not immutable like the rules of physics. There are diversities in patterns of speech and behaviour according to individual factors such as region, age, sex, social status and so on.

This book therefore deals in generalities. It does not characterise how each individual Japanese would behave in any specific situation. Such a stereotype does not exist, as each individual and each interaction is unique. The focus is, therefore, on the shared values and beliefs that are common to most Japanese.

Another point which requires attention is that cross-cultural awareness does not imply assimilation. Nor is it mimicry. Rather, it aims to foster the understanding and appreciation of different values and behaviour as they are experienced in different cultures and through different languages.

Cross-cultural Communication and Culture Shock

The point has already been made that members of a culture share scenarios that largely determine both what is appropriate behaviour in various circumstances and how to interpret the behaviour of others. Upon entering a foreign culture, people discover that the scenarios that they have learnt hitherto are suddenly invalid. In the resulting confusion, they feel awkward and helpless. Some feel as if they have been deprived of self-esteem. This bewilderment in a new environment is often called culture shock.

At first in the new environment, everything appears novel. Newcomers generously evaluate every aspect of the new culture — very often to the extent that they regard it as being better than their own. During this euphoric period, members of the new culture may pamper newcomers and take special care of them. Many short-term visitors, such as tourists or students undertaking intensive courses, may return home while still at this stage.

After a certain length of time in the new culture, that is, when life in the new environment becomes a daily reality, people expect to organise their lives just as they did at home. Then the attitude of the bank teller, the frequency of the bus services and the abruptness of members of the new culture become issues to be addressed. Newcomers compare the new situations in which they find themselves with situations in their own culture. They attempt to attach meanings to the behaviour which they encounter. Many Japanese, for example, perceive Australian egalitarianism as a lack of dignity or of manners. Some people try to explain unpleasant experiences in stereotypical terms: 'That's typical of those people …'.

This period of grievance may be accompanied by physical symptoms, such as rashes, headaches and over-eating. The phenomenon of rapid weight gain in a short time is frequently encountered. Feelings of helplessness often compel newcomers to get together with members of their own culture. In this way, they find refuge from the new culture.

The stage of bitterness is followed by a period of acceptance — 'this is the way this society operates because...'. People find a way out of despair. They realise that what is happening in the new culture is not irrational but is rather bound by its own set of cultural and social rules. In this recovery stage, newcomers make friends not only among people of the same cultural background but also among local residents who help newcomers look at situations from new perspectives. They no longer feel irritated by differences between their own culture and the new culture; rather they gain the ability to analyse situations according to either set of rules.

The degree of accommodation to the new culture varies from individual to individual. Some encounter few obstacles. Others may not escape the stage of hostility for a considerable period of time. However, whatever the individual differences and no matter what stage of adjustment the individual may be at, it is important to realise that culture shock is a universal phenomenon. It is a phenomenon that has to be coped with, and in coping, it is helpful to develop an analytical rather than a judgmental attitude towards new situations. There should be no such thing as a judgment that an action in the new culture is 'wrong'. Situations should rather be observed and analysed to answer the question 'Why is it so?'. The rest of this book is dedicated to fostering this attitude.

> At an orientation seminar for overseas students, the co-ordinator said to the newly arrived students, 'Don't look at things through your own sunglasses. When you feel lost or angry in the new society you are about to join, take off your sunglasses and look around.'
>
> What did the co-ordinator mean by 'sunglasses'?
>
> How can teachers help their students take off their sunglasses?

> From your own experiences of life in another culture, which aspects of life did you find most pleasant. Which aspects did you find most difficult to adapt to?
>
> How did you make the adjustment?
>
> What aspects of your own experience might be relevant to those of your students who are going through the same process?

> Many Japanese students come to Australia to undertake short courses, typically ranging from one to three months. Do you think their experience of culture shock would differ from that of Japanese coming to Australia for an extended period? How do you think any differences would manifest themselves?

Classroom Tasks

■ Task 1 ■

In the Macquarie Dictionary, 'culture shock' is defined as:

> 'The disorientation and unhappiness caused by an inability to adapt to a culture which is different from one's own.'

How would you define culture shock? With a partner, decide on your own definition of culture shock and write it in the space below.

Culture shock is:

Have you experienced culture shock? Describe your experiences to your partner.

Are you still experiencing culture shock? If not, how long did it take you to adjust to life in Australia?

How can you cope with culture shock? With your partner, make a list of things that might help you cope.

■ Task 2 ■

A friend is soon to arrive on a visit to Australia. This is his/her first time abroad. Write a letter describing your feelings when you first arrived in Australia.

What advice would you give to help him/her adjust quickly to Australia?

CHAPTER ■ TWO

BACKGROUND
The Land and the People

Geography

The islands of Japan extend in a bow four thousand kilometres from the northeast to the southwest, and comprise four major islands: Hokkaido, Honshu (the main island), Shikoku and Kyushu, and over three thousand smaller islands.

The 380 000 square kilometre landmass is dominated by mountains — 70 per cent of Japan consists of mountain chains which include both active and dormant volcanoes. Mount Fuji is in fact a volcano that last erupted in 1707.

Geologists believe that until the end of the last Ice Age the islands were part of the Asian continent. A rise in sea levels subsequently separated the islands from the continent and converted what were previously coastal mountain ranges into the islands of Japan.

Although the land surface is 150 per cent of that of the United Kingdom, mountain ranges and dense forests severely restrict the amount of usable land. Of the 30 per cent suitable for human occupation, 15 per cent is devoted to agriculture, 3 per cent to residential use and only 0.4 per cent for industrial purposes.

Population

Japan's population is approximately 120 million, of which 80 per cent is concentrated in the major cities. Tokyo, for example, with approximately 12 million people, comprises a tenth of the entire population.

The average rate of population growth is presently less than one per cent. At the same time, the average life span has increased remarkably, so that the average life expectancy in Japan is the highest in the world at seventy-five for men and eight-one for women.

As in many developed countries, a decline in the birth and death rates has begun to alter the population structure. By the year 2020, it is expected that one in four, or about 23.6 per cent of the population will be over sixty-five years old. As a result of such changes, there is a growing concern about the emergence of an 'ageing society'. Issues such as welfare and the shrinking working population will pose major challenges to Japanese society.

History

While Japanese history goes back as far as 100 000 years, when the Japanese archipelago was part of the Asian continent, the first evidence of a hunting and gathering culture dates back to around 8000 BC.

Wet rice cultivation was introduced from the continent around 300 BC and resulted in the emergence of a number of small states consisting of villages united by common interests such as irrigation. The division of labour entailed in the shift to settled agriculture resulted in an increasing gap between rulers and their subjects.

Around AD 200 these small states were gradually unified. The leaders of the powerful Yamamoto clan, claiming direct descent from the sun goddess, subjugated the surrounding clans and established what is known as the **Yamato Chotei** – the Imperial Court. The country was governed by an emperor who ruled with the support of court nobles.

Until the late ninth century, Japan enjoyed a remarkable period in terms of its cultural history. Delegations were sent to China, especially during the Sui and Tang dynasties, and on their return introduced Chinese art, literature and science, forming the basis of Japanese culture. Chinese ideograms were adapted to write Japanese, an innovation introduced by a Korean scholar. Buddhism took root in the sixth century and Buddhist monks from the Korean kingdom of Paekche travelled to Japan, followed by temple builders and artisans.

In 894 the decline of the Tang dynasty resulted in the discontinuation of delegations to China, although its culture was adapted and assimilated to form the features characteristic of Japanese culture. One of the most significant examples of the way an initial Chinese input was transformed is the development of **kana** or the syllabaries which were made by simplifying Chinese ideograms. Two syllabaries were developed, **hiragana** and **katakana**. The chart below illustrates the process of change that resulted in **hiragana**.

Development of Kana

a	安	-- 安 --	あ
i	以	-- 以 --	い
u	宇	-- 宇 --	う
e	衣	-- 衣 --	え
o	於	-- 於 --	お

The Rise of the Warrior Class

Until the twelfth century, Japan was ruled by emperors and court nobles. Regional clans were appointed to lower bureaucratic positions and were responsible for the administration of military power. Gradually these clans developed into a warrior class, the ***samurai***. The nobility was thus split into the civilian nobles of the court and the ***samurai*** who wielded military power. Power increasingly passed to the military, and the emperor was gradually deprived of political and economic influence. However, both the emperor and the court nobles who surrounded him continued to be socially respected.

In 1192, the Minamoto family established the shogunate or military government. Minamoto Yoritomo, on being appointed shogun or military ruler, transferred the administrative capital to Kamakura, near present-day Tokyo, while the titular government, that is the emperor and his court, remained in Kyoto. Thus established, the ***samurai*** retained political power until the late nineteenth century. Initially, several powerful families contested the shogunate and it was not until Tokugawa Ieyasu established the Tokugawa shogunate in 1603 and put an end to the period of 'warring states' that a lasting peace was obtained. The shogunate founded by Ieyasu lasted 260 years, during which time fourteen successors acceded to Ieyasu's position.

In order to maintain its rule, the Tokugawa shogunate implemented various policies aimed at depriving both the masses and the feudal lords of their power. Most importantly, they enforced a four-fold hierarchy onto society, dividing it into the ***shi*** (samurai), ***noo*** (peasants), ***koo*** (artisans) and ***shoo*** (merchants). In enforcing this hierarchical system, the shogunate intended to prevent merchants from attaining economic dominance and to limit social mobility.

Another effective instrument of control was the ***sankinkootai***, whereby feudal lords were required to visit the seat of the Tokugawa central government in Edo (modern Tokyo) almost every year. At the same time, their families were required to reside in Edo. This obligation to travel to the capital bringing hundreds of retainers brought wealth to the shogunate while effectively depleting the resources of the feudal lords. At the same time, their loyalty was assured by the fact that their families were virtual hostages.

A policy of national isolation was declared for fear that the provincial lords in the southwest region would become economically powerful through foreign trade. This was allied to a desire to limit contact with foreign countries, whose military and ideological influence was feared. Similarly, Christianity was banned because of its concepts of equality and freedom, and to prevent the emergence of any movement counter to the prevailing neo-Confucian political ideology. Japan was thus isolated from the rest of the world, except for some limited trade with China, the Netherlands and Korea conducted through the southern port of Nagasaki. It was at this time that such characteristic Japanese cultural activities as **Kabuki** (drama) and **Ukiyoe** (woodblock printing) reached their peak.

The Meiji Restoration

During the late eighteenth and the beginning of the nineteenth centuries, Japan encountered increasing demands from foreign countries to open its doors. Domestically, the rigid social and political system began to collapse as the merchant class became powerful through the development of a monetary economy.

In 1854 the shogunate finally accepted demands by the American envoy, Commodore Perry, for a treaty of amity with the United States. Similar treaties were rapidly concluded with Britain, Russia, France and the Netherlands.

In 1868, political power was returned to the emperor, or, more accurately, to a group of reformers who acted in his name. The following period, known as the Meiji Restoration after the Meiji emperor, was one of rapid change. The emperor transferred his seat to Edo, the centre of the shogunate and renamed it Tokyo, the 'Eastern Capital'. He announced a program of five articles, pledging a centralised parliamentary government, and the abolition of the class system. Some feudal lords were, however, able to maintain their positions. A constitution was promulgated in 1889 and new policies such as conscription and monetary taxation introduced. During the Edo period, taxes had been paid in kind.

Modern industries were founded and Western thought and institutions exerted a tremendous influence. Many Japanese felt ashamed at the 'backwardness' of Japanese technology and culture. One result was that precious artworks such as the scrolls containing the great eleventh century novel Tales of Genji were cut up and sold off to Western collectors at derisory prices. However, by the 1880s this feeling had been replaced by a conviction that while Japan could indeed learn a great deal from the west in the realms of science and technology, in terms of culture Japan could easily hold its own.

Modern Japan

The new era heralded the growth of industry. In the late nineteenth century the first phase of the industrial revolution took place with the development of light industry, especially textiles. The second phase, centring on heavy industries such as ship-building and steel manufacturing, rapidly followed.

Meanwhile, the Sino-Japanese War (1894-95) and the Russo-Japanese War (1904-05) took place, reflecting a growing interest in market expansion after the development of industrial power. Victory in both wars encouraged nationalism, which was reinforced by a reaction against the feeling of inferiority in relation to the West. A growing confidence in the strength of the nation and an increasing economic interest in expansion into Asia ushered in the period of imperialism.

In the early twentieth century, during the reign of the Taisho emperor (1912-26), successor to the Meiji emperor, Japan participated in the First World War as a result of the Anglo-Japanese Alliance. Japan's main interest in co-operating with the Allies, and especially with Russia and England, was to expand into new markets on the Asian continent. Through the Treaty of Versailles, signed in 1919, Japan gained control of Chinese territory, including the Shandong peninsula, and became a member of the Council of the League of Nations. In China, anti-Japanese feeling exploded among university students in Beijing, leading to demonstrations and boycotts of Japanese goods.

Meanwhile, the **zaibatsu** were strengthening their position and gaining control of capital-based industries. **Zaibatsu** were family-based corporations such as Mitsui and Mitsubishi which, by forming networks of affiliated companies, were able to dominate industry and the economy. Their wealth, initially founded in textile manufacturing, was now invested in heavy industry and munitions and their operations proved very successful, especially after World War 1, when they were able to take over Germany's former markets in Asia. The **zaibatsu**, which had a close relationship with the government, tended to support Japan's move towards imperialism.

Domestically, inflation was rampant. Since the beginning of the First World War the workers, unlike the small number of bourgeoisie, had suffered severely from reduced wages and the increased price of rice. War expenditures financed by means of such sacrifice aroused great anger. In response to this suffering and also because of the influence of the Russian revolution, various socialist organisations were formed. This influenced the granting of male suffrage in 1925.

During this turbulent period the Great Kanto Earthquake of 1923 caused the deaths of 100 000 people and demolished large sections of Tokyo. Panicking citizens massacred many Korean residents, accusing them of having poisoned the water supply, and the military were able to take advantage of the resulting turmoil to assassinate several anarchists and other left-wing figures.

Towards the Second World War

In 1926 the Showa era began with the accession of the Showa emperor (Hirohito). The worldwide depression and its effect on the nation's economic life accelerated a growing distrust of politicians. Under these circumstances, the power of the military increased as key government portfolios fell into their hands and the country moved to the right. Freedom of speech was curtailed.

In 1931, the Japanese Kwantung Army stationed in China occupied the whole of Manchuria and established the puppet regime of Manchukuo headed by the last emperor of China. This action was internationally criticised, and as a result Japan withdrew from the League of Nations. Having taken Manchuria, Japan continued to expand south, and in 1937, in the capture of Nanking (present-day Nanjing), tens of thousands of civilians were massacred.

Domestically, a coup d'etat attempted by a group of young military officers who wanted to restore absolute power to the emperor resulted in the deaths of several cabinet members. In the wake of this incident, the military tightened its control on power.

In response to fears about present and future Japanese expansion into east and southeast Asia, the United States put pressure on Japan by freezing the assets owned by Japanese-Americans and by prohibiting trade in munitions. Increasing tension culminated in the Japanese attack on Pearl Harbour, an attack that was intended to neutralise the US navy. War broke out between the United States and Japan.

A rapid advance left Japan in control of Indo-China, Malaya, Indonesia, the Philippines, most of Burma and many of the Pacific Islands. However, by 1944, the war proved unwinnable for Japan. Munitions factories and industrial areas, as well as residential neighbourhoods, were widely demolished by air raids. The US army landed in Okinawa and invasion of the main islands was imminent. In desperation, kamikaze squadrons were formed to lead suicide attacks on enemy shipping.

In May 1945, the war in Europe ended with Germany's unconditional surrender. A dispute took place within the Japanese government on whether or not Japan should itself surrender. Many cabinet members feared that the position of the emperor might be compromised by such a surrender. Meanwhile, immediately prior to the Soviet Union's entry into the Pacific theatre of the war, the United States attempted to bring the war to a rapid conclusion. On the sixth of August, Hiroshima was attacked with a nuclear bomb. This was followed by the attack on Nagasaki on the ninth of August. Japan surrendered unconditionally.

Post-War Japan

The Allied occupation under General MacArthur saw many reforms, including land reform, which involved the redistribution of the property of the landowners to the peasantry and the dismantling of the *zaibatsu*, the industrial conglomerates. A new constitution was drafted which guaranteed basic human rights such as education and suffrage. Women were granted the right to vote soon after.

The Japanese Empire thus came to an end. The emperor publicly denied his position as a 'Living God' and became instead the symbol of the state. With the signing of the San Francisco Peace Treaty between the United States and Japan in 1951, Japan resumed its role in the international community.

The Korean War, which started in 1950, brought economic prosperity to Japan. Munitions supplies ordered by the United States provided the foundation for Japan's rapid economic growth in the 1950s. In 1968, Japan's GNP became the second highest in the world. Japan's rapid economic development, however, came to an end when OPEC quadrupled the price of oil in 1972. The so-called 'oil-shock' underlined the vulnerability of Japan's position, since it is a country with extremely limited natural resources. The economy shifted from one of rapid growth to one of more steady output.

In the 1970s and 1980s, Japan's policy of protectionism was internationally criticised, resulting in the review of her export-based trade policies. Meanwhile, the NICs (the Newly Industrialised Countries: Korea, Taiwan, Hong Kong and Singapore) entered Japan's traditional markets. Japan shifted her focus from labour intensive industries to high-tech industries.

However, Japan's post-war prosperity has been bought at considerable cost. For example, the age of industrialisation has neglected primary industries in the rural areas. Depopulation in those regions is a serious problem, in that many villages in remote areas no longer have sufficient population to sustain themselves. Consequently, continuation of the old tradition is now under threat. Economic success has also created serious pollution problems. In the process of rebuilding its land and its economy, Japan has neglected the environmental damage caused by industrial waste. Chemical pollution has resulted in disasters such as **minamata** disease, caused by mercury poisoning. Japan in the post-industrial age must not only come to terms with the problems created domestically as the result of prosperity, but must also, as a developed nation, pursue her responsibilities internationally.

Government

Japan is a constitutional monarchy whose government comprises three independent branches, the legislative, the executive and the judicial. The Diet or the Legislature is divided into the House of Representatives and the House of Councillors, to both of which members are directly elected. The Diet also has the power to elect the Prime Minister and to dismiss both Prime Ministers and Ministers.

According to the constitution, the emperor is the ceremonial and diplomatic Head of State. He also performs such functions as appointing the Chief Justice of the Supreme Court in consultation with the cabinet.

Most Diet members belong to political parties, the most important of which are the Liberal Democratic Party, the Democratic Socialist Party, the Communist Party and Komeito, a party with Buddhist links. The Liberal Democratic Party has won every election since it was formed in 1955. The political picture is, however, complicated by the existence of well-organised factions within the parties. These factions play an important role. It is the factional leaders, for example, who effectively nominate the prime minister.

Religion

Today the role of religion in Japan is more a cultural than a religious one. Just as in Australia, where the celebration of Christmas often tends to be divorced from religious practice, so in Japan religious activities such as **hatsumoode**, a Shintoist traditional in which people visit the temple at the beginning of the year to pray for well-being and good health, tend to be performed without any particular religious awareness. This does not mean, however, that Japanese are non-religious. In fact, according to official statistics, the religious population is much larger than the actual population. This is because many Japanese consider themselves to be both Shintoist and Buddhist.

Culturally, Buddhism and Shinto co-exist in harmony. Shinto is the indigenous religion of Japan. In its rituals, **Kami** (spirits), consisting of animistic deities such as the spirits of mountains and rivers and the souls of heroes and outstanding leaders, are enshrined and worshipped. When Buddhism was introduced into Japan, it assimilated many aspects of Shinto, with Shinto spirits being seen as incarnations of the Buddha. Both religions lay heavy emphasis on ancestor worship, and it is this, rather than the more abstract principles of religious belief, that is important to most Japanese.

The dual acknowledgement of Buddhism and Shinto means that many Japanese households contain both a **kamidana**, a family Shinto altar, and a **Butsudan**, a family Buddhist altar. Similarly, many Japanese go through Shinto rites when they marry and Buddhist rites when they die.

Christians are also active, with Protestants outnumbering Catholics. However, numbers are small, less than one per cent of the population and Christianity is generally viewed as a foreign religion, whereas Buddhism no longer is.

Under the constitution, religion and politics are separate. Nevertheless, there have been several controversies regarding the attitude of the government toward Shinto. The Yasukuni shrine, for example, enshrines the souls of deceased soldiers. Every year many politicians officially visit the shrine. Some people object to this, claiming that it violates the constitution and has military connotations. Others claim that a visit to the shrine is simply to appease the souls of the deceased who died fighting for their country.

CHAPTER ■ THREE

FEATURES OF THE JAPANESE LANGUAGE

In this chapter we will outline some of the features of the Japanese language that are of particular significance in relation to language learning.

The Japanese Sound System

Many English language teachers comment that the English their Japanese learners speak sounds monotonous. Some teachers have the impression that their students tend to chop off their words when speaking English. In this section we will seek explanations for these characteristics.

Phonemes and Syllables

There are basically five vowels, two semi-vowels and fifteen consonants in Japanese phonology, roughly represented as follows:

Vowels: /a/ /i/ /u/ /e/ /o/
Semi-vowels: /w/ /y/
Consonants: /k/ /g/ /s/ /z/ /t/ /c/ /d/
/n/ /h/ /b/ /p/ /m/ /r/ /N/ /Q/

However, some consonants change their pronunciation according to the vowels that follow them. The following examples give a rough idea of what happens:

Pronunciation	Pronunciation
s + a = sa	z + a = za
s + i = <u>shi</u>	z + i = <u>ji</u>
s + u = su	z + u = zu
s + e = se	z + e = ze
s + o = so	z + o = zo

Most syllables comprise a combination of a consonant and a vowel. This C-V structure is an important feature of Japanese and words are usually composed of C-V units, though some syllables comprise a single vowel only:

| ga + ku + se + i | gakusei | 'a student' |
| ku + ru + ma | kuruma | 'a car' |

Some of the major differences between Japanese and English phonology are, first of all, that Japanese has a vowel 'u', which is pronounced with the lips unrounded. The 'r' sound is pronounced with the tongue curled back and touching the hard palate. This means that it has a certain similarity both to an English 'd' and to an English 'l'. Japanese learners often fail to distinguish between an 'l' and an 'r' in listening to and speaking English, while English speaking learners of Japanese often have difficulty in distinguishing the Japanese 'r' and 'd'.

Mora (Stress) and Pitch

In the previous section we discussed how a Japanese syllable is composed of a consonant and a vowel. This feature often interferes with a learner's pronunciation of foreign languages:

yotto	'a yacht'
chokoleeto	'a chocolate'

'Yacht', for example, often tends to be pronounced 'yo-t-to'. The explanation for this lies in the C-V structure of Japanese syllables. Learners often add a vowel after a word-final consonant to give the syllable a C-V structure. Some Japanese learners may, however, over-react when they realise that English does not have a C-V structure. One learner, determined to improve his pronunciation, decided that he should delete all word final vowels. He was surprised and puzzled when English speakers did not recognise what a 'mosquit' was!

Also, Japanese does not place variable stress on syllables as English does. Each syllable is pronounced independently and with the same stress. You may in fact have noticed that your Japanese learners tend to ignore stress differences in English. Furthermore, Japanese gives equal status to each consonant in a double consonant or to each vowel where a vowel only syllable follows a C-V syllable. This means that the first "t" in 'yotto' is treated separately from the second "t", and also that the first "t" is glottally stopped because of the C-V structure, so the word is pronounced 'yo-t-to' as represented above. Other examples, this time taken from Japanese, are:

kitte	'a stamp'	'ki-t-te'
yuubinkyoku	'a post office'	'yu-u-bi-n-kyo-ku'
onna	'a woman'	'o-n-na'

As with Japanese speakers learning English, so English speakers learning Japanese are influenced by their native stress when learning Japanese. An English speaker's pronunciation of the above words would probably be 'kiteh', 'yubinkyoku' and 'ona'. At the same time, stress would be placed on one syllable and the following syllable shortened. This would maintain the English speech rhythm.

The name given to this tendency to give every syllable equal time is *mora*.

The role of *mora* in Japanese is evident in the treatment of English words adapted into the language, an example of which we have already seen. A further example is the word **koohii**, 'coffee'. It is broken into syllables of equal length according to mora and pronounced 'ko-o-hi-i'.

You may wonder at this point how Japanese coin vocabulary when the number of possible syllables is limited by the requirements of the C-V structure. In fact, Japanese is full of homonyms. In the written language, use of **kanji** distinguishes differences in meaning. Words that sound the same are written differently. In the spoken language, however, pitch plays an important role in distinguishing between words that have a similar pronunciation. Here are several examples:

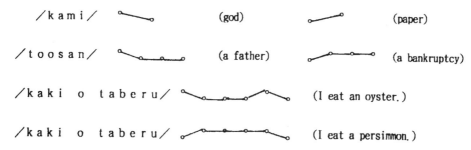

/k a m i/   (god)   (paper)

/t o o s a n/   (a father)   (a bankruptcy)

/k a k i o t a b e r u/   (I eat an oyster.)

/k a k i o t a b e r u/   (I eat a persimmon.)

Kami, when pronounced with a high pitch on 'ka' and a low pitch on 'mi' means 'god', while a low pitch on 'ka' and a high pitch on 'mi' means 'paper'. However, Japanese is not a tonal language, and there are regional differences in pitch which mean that a person from western Japan ordering persimmons in Tokyo may in fact get oysters!

Can you provide phonological explanations for the following problems?

★ Mariko is disappointed when she orders her favourite vanilla icecream at the shop. She always gets given banana.
Can   I   have   vanilla   icecream?
'Kyan ai   ha-bu   ba-ni-ra   ai-su-kri-i-mu'

★ Steven was in Japan for six months as an exchange student. One day he asked the way to the hospital, **byooin**. After following the directions, he found himself in front of the hairdressers, **biyooin**.

> The following are English words borrowed by the Japanese. Ask your Japanese students to pronounce them and see how they have been adapted into the Japanese phonological system:
>
> | | |
> |---|---|
> | *kompyuutaa* | 'a computer' |
> | *suupaamaaketto* | 'a supermarket' |
> | *handobaggu* | 'a handbag' |

The Japanese Writing System

Japanese writing consists of **kana**, which comprise two separate phonetic alphabets called respectively **hiragana** and **katakana**, and **kanji**, which are Chinese ideograms. In modern Japanese, **katakana** is mainly used for foreign words adapted into Japanese and occasionally for onomatapoeic words. Otherwise, **hiragana** is used. The table on pages 24-25 sets out the **hiragana** alphabet.

Kana form the basis of Japanese writing. A sequence of **kana** forms a word:

とけい　(a watch)

えいご　(English)

In addition to **kana**, Japanese writing also uses kanji, ideographs which were adopted from China during the sixth century AD. Each kanji carries a basic meaning but has several different pronunciations. When kanji were adopted into Japanese, they were used to write already existing Japanese words, that is, words that already had their own pronunciation. So each **kanji** could be read according to its original Chinese pronunciation or according to its Japanese language pronunciation. For example, the **kanji** written 山 is translated as 'mountain' in English. In Japanese, it has two different pronunciations. Firstly, it can be pronounced 'yama', which is the original Japanese word for 'mountain'. However, it can also be pronounced 'san' in words such as **sanmyaku**, 山脈 which are borrowed from Chinese.

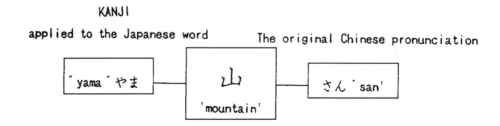

Similarly, 友, 'friend' is pronounced 'tomo', but at the same time can be pronounced 'yuujin' when it occurs in words such as 友人 borrowed from the Chinese. These semantically similar words are used in different contexts and registers.

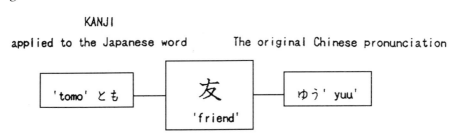

Japanese sentences can be written using only kana and in fact young children start to learn to write this way. Nevertheless, in normal writing, **kana** and **kanji** are combined. Words that relate to concepts, actions and things, such as nouns, verbs and adjectives are written in **kanji**, while **kana** are used for grammatical items such as particles and auxiliary verbs.

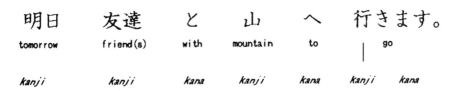

ashita tomodachi to yama e ikimasu
tomorrow friends with mountain to go (non-past)
'Tomorrow I will go to the mountains with friends.'

KANA (hiragana)

	a	i	u	e	o
	あ a	い i	う u	え e	お o
k	か ka	き ki	く ku	け ke	こ ko
s	さ sa	し shi	す su	せ se	そ so
t	た ta	ち chi	つ tsu	て te	と to
n	な na	に ni	ぬ nu	ね ne	の no
h	は ha	ひ hi	ふ hu	へ he	ほ ho
m	ま ma	み mi	む mu	め me	も mo
y	や ya	(い) i	ゆ yu	(え) e	よ yo
r	ら ra	り ri	る ru	れ re	ろ ro
w	わ wa	(い) i	(う) u	(え) e	を wo
g	が ga	ぎ gi	ぐ gu	げ ge	ご go
z	ざ za	じ ji	ず zu	ぜ ze	ぞ zo
d	だ da	ぢ ji	づ zu	で de	ど do
b	ば ba	び bi	ぶ bu	べ be	ぼ bo
p	ぱ pa	ぴ pi	ぷ pu	ぺ pe	ぽ po
N	ん n				

FEATURES OF THE JAPANESE LANGUAGE

py	by	zy(j)	gy	ry	my	hy	ny	cy(ch)	sy(sh)	ky	
ぴゃ pya	びゃ bya	じゃ ja	ぎゃ gya	りゃ rya	みゃ mya	ひゃ hya	にゃ nya	ちゃ cha	しゃ sha	きゃ kya	a
ぴゅ pyu	びゅ byu	じゅ ju	ぎゅ gyu	りゅ ryu	みゅ myu	ひゅ hyu	にゅ nyu	ちゅ chu	しゅ shu	きゅ kyu	u
ぴょ pyo	びょ byo	じょ jo	ぎょ gyo	りょ ryo	みょ myo	ひょ hyo	にょ nyo	ちょ cho	しょ sho	きょ kyo	o

Japanese Grammar

The following paragraphs describe how Japanese grammar is structured.

Particles

The following is a key to the abbreviations used to indicate the parts of speech:

>Subject marker: Sub
>Direct Object marker: D Obj
>Indirect Object or Receiver: In Obj
>Particle: P

Japanese belongs to the family of agglutinative languages, in that particles are added to the end of each word to indicate the word's semantic function. Unlike English, which basically follows a Subject-Verb-Object (SVO) structure, Japanese basically has a Subject-Object-Verb (SOV) structure.

>*sensei   wa   gakusei   ni   eigo   o   oshiemasu*
>teacher P-Sub student P-In Obj English P-Ob teach
> S | O | V

'The teacher teaches the student English'

>   S | V | In Obj   D Obj
>
>*gakusei   ni   sensei   wa   eigo   o   oshiemasu*
>student P-In Obj teacher P-Sub English P-D Obj teach
>   O | S | O | V

'The teacher teaches the student English'

As the above examples reveal, it is the particles placed after the words rather than the word order that carry the semantic load.

The following sentences provide further examples of the significance of particles in Japanese:

>*Neko   wa   nezumi   o   oikakemashita*
>   P-Sub   P-Obj
>cat   mouse .   to chase (past)

'The cat chased the mouse'.

>*Nezumi   o   neko   wa   oikakemashita*
>   P-Obj   P-Sub
>mouse   cat   to chase(past)

'The cat chased the mouse'.

In these two sentences, the word order is different, but the semantic value remains the same because the particles which follow subject and object are not changed. The basic logic of the sentence is therefore not determined by word order.

Auxiliaries

We have already examined the basic structure of Japanese, in the sense of who did what. However, we also need to be able to modify our ideas,to express shades of meaning. In English, many of these shades of meaning are expressed by auxiliary verbs such as 'should', 'may' and 'might':

I *might* go if I have time.

Japanese expresses these shades of meaning by adding auxiliary elements to the ends of verbs:

Sensei   wa   ashita   kuru
Teacher   P-Sub   tomorrow   come (non-past)
'The teacher (will) come tomorrow.'

Sensei   wa   ashita   kurudeshoo
Teacher   P-Sub   tomorrow   come (non-past) perhaps
'The teacher may come tomorrow.'

Deshoo added to the plain verb expresses the speaker's estimation of possibility. Here are some further examples:

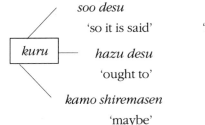

soo desu	*Kazuko wa ashita kurusoodesu*
'so it is said'	'Apparently, Kazuko will come tomorrow.'
hazu desu	*Kazuko wa ashita kuruhazudesu*
'ought to'	'Kazuko ought to come tomorrow.'
kamo shiremasen	*Kazuko wa asita kurukamoshiremasen*
'maybe'	'Kazuko will probably come tomorrow.'

Auxiliary elements also express the action of the verb in relation to time. Japanese basically marks whether the action described in a verb is complete or incomplete. It also marks the duration of an action. These distinctions are roughly similar to the difference between the English 'I have read the book', where the action is completed, and 'I am reading the book', where the action is represented as on-going or as having duration.

Here are some examples of such auxiliaries in Japanese:

tori   ga   shinimashita
bird   P-Sub   die (past)
'The bird died.'

tori   ga   shinde   imasu
bird P-Sub die: te form exist
              (connective)
'The bird is dead.'

The verb **shinimashita** denotes the moment of dying. The change in the form of the principal verb and the addition of **imasu**, which roughly translates as 'state of being/existing', extends the meaning of the verb by treating it as a permanent state.

Other auxiliaries can be used in the same way:

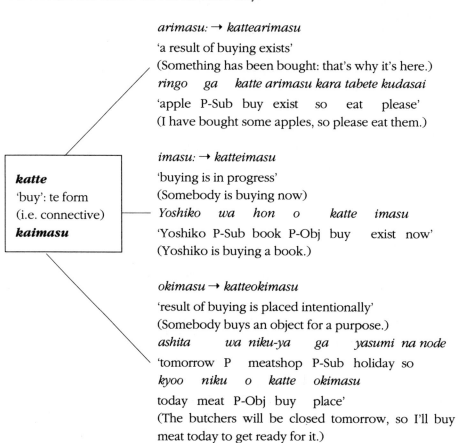

arimasu: → *kattearimasu*
'a result of buying exists'
(Something has been bought: that's why it's here.)
ringo   ga   katte arimasu kara tabete kudasai
'apple P-Sub buy   exist   so   eat   please'
(I have bought some apples, so please eat them.)

imasu: → *katteimasu*
'buying is in progress'
(Somebody is buying now)
Yoshiko   wa   hon   o   katte   imasu
'Yoshiko P-Sub book P-Obj buy   exist now'
(Yoshiko is buying a book.)

okimasu → *katteokimasu*
'result of buying is placed intentionally'
(Somebody buys an object for a purpose.)
ashita   wa   niku-ya   ga   yasumi na node
'tomorrow   P   meatshop P-Sub holiday so
kyoo   niku   o   katte   okimasu
today   meat P-Obj   buy   place'
(The butchers will be closed tomorrow, so I'll buy meat today to get ready for it.)

katte
'buy': te form
(i.e. connective)
kaimasu

Subject v Topic Orientation

One of the distinctive features of Japanese syntax is its topic-comment orientation. The speaker tends to state the topic of the sentence and then make a comment or give some information about that topic. Here are some examples:

Ano resutoran wa saabisu ga ii desu
Topic | Comment
that restaurant P-Sub service P-Sub good copula (polite)
　　　　Topic marker　　　Comment marker
'As for that restaurant, the service is good.'

Taroh-san wa tenisu ga joozu desu
Topic | Comment
Taroh　　P-Sub tennis　P-Sub skilful　copula (polite)
　　　Topic marker　Comment marker
'As for Taro, he is good at tennis.'

Sidonii wa kankookyaku ga ooi
Topic | Comment
Sydney P-Sub tourists P-Sub plenty
　　Topic marker　Comment marker
'As for Sydney, there are many tourists.'

In choosing the topic, there is also a strong tendency to describe events as they affect the speaker. This contrasts with the English tendency to describe events from the point of view of an outsider. If you are watching a football match and the person sitting next to you, caught up in the excitement of the game, spills his beer all over you, you are likely to explain why you are wet by saying, in English, something like 'A man spilled his beer on me.' In Japanese, the same event would more likely be reported as:

watashi wa otokonohito ni biiru o kakeraremashita
　　Topic | Comment
　I　P-Sub　a man　P-In Obj　beer P-D Obj spill:past passive
'I had beer spilled on me by a man'

The sentence describes the happening as it affects the speaker. On following page are some further examples of this 'speaker-orientated' tendency together with an English gloss.

watashi wa jooshi ni shigoto o tanomaremashita.
(As for me, my boss asked me to do the work.)

watashi wa ame ni huraremashita. — watashi 'I' — *watashi wa inu ni kamaremashita.*
(As for me, it rained.)   (As for me, a dog bit me.)

watashi wa tomodachi ni nakaremashita.
(As for me, my friend cried on me.)

topic   comment

WATASHI WA
'I'

jooshi ni shigoto o tanomaremashita
(had my boss ask to do the job.)
ame ni huraremashita
(it rained and I suffered.)
tomodachi ni nakaremashita
(had my friend cry on me and I was troubled.)
inu ni te o kamaremashita
(had my hand bitten by a dog.)

Topic and Comment in Japanese

Expressing Time

A language portrays the way that the outside world is perceived by its speakers. Different languages represent the world in different ways, and one area of difference concerns the way that time is viewed. Japanese assumptions about temporality may affect a student's selection of tense in English, so it is worth briefly examining these assumptions.

Look at the following conversation between Goro and Hajime who are planning a holiday in Tasmania:

Goro: *Debunpooto ni tsuitara kuruma kariyoo ka?*
Devonport P-Loc arrive (past cond) car hire:vol P-int
'Will we hire a car when we arrive in Devonport?'

Hajime: *Un soo shiyoo*
yeah so do: vol
'Yeah, let's do that.'

Loc — Location
Cond — Conditional
Vol — Volitional
Int — Interrogative

Notice that the English gloss uses the present tense 'arrive', whereas the Japanese marks the verb as past. Goro refers to their arrival in Devonport as past because he visualises the time scale like this:

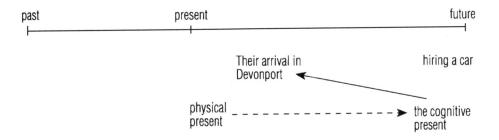

He sees the future event of 'arriving in Devonport' from the perspective of the event 'hiring a car'. From this perspective, the event in the subordinate clause, 'arriving in Devonport' is in the past. The speaker is not relating time to the physical time of speaking but to a 'cognitive present'. He takes an imagined time in the future and uses that as the baseline of his judgement of past.

Another important point is the way duration is conceptualised. States and habitual actions are both treated as continuations of an initial action. So, for example, take the following sentence:

mado   ga   warete   imasu
window P-Sub break   exist
'The window is broken.'

The action 'break' is treated as a continuing state by the addition of ***imasu***. In other words, the nearest English gloss would be something like 'the window breaks and continues in that broken state'.

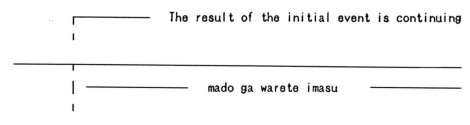

Another example, this time involving what in English would be an habitual action, is as follows:

Sachiko-san   wa   pan-ya   de   hataraite   imasu
Sachiko title P-Sub   bakery   P-Loc   work   exist
'Sachiko works in a bakery.'

'Work' is seen as a continuing state, just as the window is in a continuing state of brokenness. This continuing state is signalled by the use of ***imasu***.

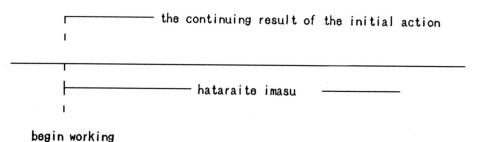

Japanese Honorifics

Tom, an exchange student, had been in Japan for almost one year and was becoming more confident about his Japanese. But one day he was upset by the reaction from his host-sister Yoko when he gave her a birthday present. He knew that the Japanese word for giving was **yarimasu**, so he very proudly said **yarimasu** as he gave her the present. In spite of the gift, Yoko seemed angry. As Tom looked puzzled, she said, 'So you think I'm inferior to you, do you? After all, you're younger than me'.

In Japanese, there are several sets of words depicting the same action. These words are used in different situations, depending on the age and status of the participants.

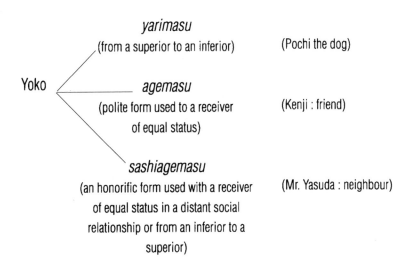

Yarimasu, **agemasu** and **sashiagemasu** realise the same action, giving. In order to interact in society, however, a person has to select the most appropriate register according to who the listener is. As is shown in the chart, the verb **yarimasu**, if used by Yoko to Mr Yasuda, would be inappropriate as it is an expression used by a superior to an inferior. Likewise, it would be inappropriate to use **sashiagemasu**, an honorific expression, to a dog. Knowing how to select the appropriate level is necessary in order to function within a speech community. What then governs such choices in Japanese? There are three major considerations:

Age

In Japanese society a great degree of respect is paid to age. The choice of speech level accordingly reflects this. Even in school situations, a junior student employs a polite form when speaking to a student from Year 11 or year 12. A more direct form is used in reply.

Status

Status refers to the hierarchical relationship that exists between socially determined roles such as manager and secretary, teacher and student, or doctor and patient. It does not refer to class relationships. The relative status of people affects the choice of speech level.

Social Distance

Social distance refers to the degree of familiarity between speaker and hearer. Polite forms which indicate considerable social distance tend to be used when people meet for the first time. The social distance between friends tends to be much less and the more direct language used between friends reflects this.

Honorific expressions are, of course, not unique to Japanese — they are used in any language where a power relationship between speaker and listener exists. English speakers also employ honorific expressions, such as 'could you', 'would you mind, possibly ...' and many others to indicate deference. The crucial difference between English and Japanese is that the use of honorifics in Japanese is based on a permanent status relationship between participants. Look at the following conversation, in which a company manager asks the secretary to type some documents:

Japanese:
Manager: *Kore taipu shite* — Direct form
 this type   do
Secretary: *Hai, kashikomarimashita* — Humble form
 yes, understand (past)
English:
Manager: Could you type this, please? — Polite form
Secretary: Certainly. — Polite form

In the English version, although the manager has a higher status than the secretary, he employs a polite form because he is the requester. In other words, the degree of politeness is determined by the position the participants are taking — here requester and requestee. In Japanese, the fixed status relationship between the two determines the use of honorific forms.

However, when talking about her manager to a third party, the secretary's use of register may alter:

Company client: *Yamada-buchoo   o   onegai shimasu*
Yamada-General Manager P-D Obj favour do
'Is Mr Yamada in?'

Secretary: *Yamada   wa   ima   gaishutsu   shite   orimasu ga*
Yamada   P-Sub now   out   do   exist (humble)
'Yamada is out of the office.'

Here, the secretary who earlier used the polite form while addressing Mr Yamada, uses a humble form when referring to him to a third party, the company client. The diagram below illustrates what happens:

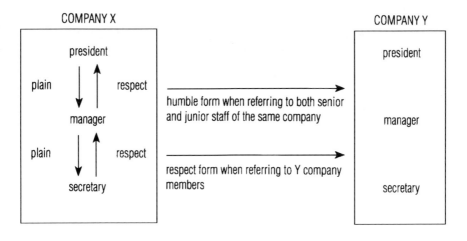

An employee of one company is expected to use the humble form when speaking to an employee of a different company. Even when a secretary is referring to the president of her company, the same rule applies, although, were she to address him directly, she would use the polite form. The reasons for this are taken up in greater detail on p. 45.

> Of the various aspects of Japanese discussed in this chapter, which do you think might most inhibit the learning of the English language?

> To what extent do you think a teacher should explicitly contrast English and Japanese in the classroom?

> When does English require politeness or deference?
>
> How aware are your students of its expression in English? Are they able to use polite forms in appropriate contexts?
>
> Look at the textbooks you commonly use in class. How do they treat the issue of politeness or deference and its use in appropriate contexts?
>
> In view of Japanese students' expectations about deference, do you think the treatment is adequate?
>
> If not, how would you supplement it?

FEATURES OF THE JAPANESE LANGUAGE

Classroom Tasks

■ Task 1 ■

A student wants to borrow a book from each of the people listed in the diagram below. In pairs, discuss how you would ask each person, first in English then in Japanese. Write what you would say in each case in the space provided.

NB: The number in brackets represents the age of the person.

```
                        ┌─────────────┐
                        │   Student   │
                        │ close friend│
                        │    (25)     │
                        └─────────────┘
┌─────────────┐    (E) _____    ┌─────────────┐
│   Student   │        _____    │   Teacher   │
│acquaintance │                             │    (43)     │
│    (25)     │    (J) _____    └─────────────┘
└─────────────┘

(E) _____   _____    (E) _____

                        ┌─────────────┐
                        │   Student   │
(J) _____    │    (23)     │    (J) _____
                        └─────────────┘
                        
_____        _____    _____

┌─────────────┐         ┌─────────────┐    ┌─────────────┐
│   Student   │         │   Student   │    │   Teacher   │
│acquaintance │         │    (18)     │    │    (43)     │
│    (25)     │         │close friend │    └─────────────┘
└─────────────┘         └─────────────┘
(E) _____    (E) _____    (E) _____

_____        _____        _____

(J) _____    (J) _____    (J) _____

_____        _____        _____
```

What differences do you notice?
Explain the differences to your teacher.

■ Task 2 ■

What would a student say if he or she wanted to borrow:

i) a pencil from a person ten years older than you?

ii) a pencil from a person of your own age?

iii) a cassette recorder from a person ten years older than you?

iv) a cassette recorder from a person your own age?

In pairs, create a dialogue for each of these four situations.

Your teacher will check to see that you are speaking appropriately.

What most affects how polite you have to be — the age difference between people or the difference in what you are asking for?

CHAPTER ■ FOUR

DEFINING SELF IN SOCIETY

Knowing one's place in society is crucial for appropriate communication to take place. Self-identification determines how one relates to other members of society and also influences the roles one adopts.

In cross-cultural communication, the definition of 'self' may differ among participants in an interaction. Signals may often be misinterpreted, resulting in unfortunate misunderstandings. Ways of addressing others, for example, vary greatly from culture to culture and what is acceptable in one may be unacceptable in others.

This chapter will examine some aspects of how Japanese identify themselves and how they relate to their families and friends.

Names

In Japanese, the family name comes first, followed by the given name. There is no custom of giving middle names.

Ooyama Yooko 大山　葉子
Tanaka Eizo 田中　栄三

Surnames are generally based on **kanji** and relate to natural surroundings or an ancestor's status or occupation. Tanaka, 田中 for example, means 'in the rice field' and Ooyama 大山 'a large mountain', which depicts the main geographical feature of the area where a person's forebears lived.

There are at present approximately 10 000 Japanese family names, but until the Meiji Restoration commoners were not allowed to have surnames.

Given names are selected according to the hopes the parents have for the child's future, or according to the season of the child's birth. For example, the name, 栄三 Eizo, records the wish for prosperity in the use of the **kanji** 栄, prosperity or honour. 三 is an ending used in boys' names. In the name 葉子, Yooko, 葉 represents a seasonal feature, 'leaves'. 子 is a typical ending used in girls' names.

Addresses

In Japanese, addresses are written in the reverse order to English.

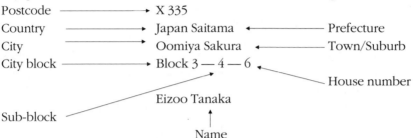

When an official document is required, such as a passport or a curriculum vitae, two addresses often have to be provided: the home address and the registered address.

The registered address, **honseki**, is the address that is entered in the census register. Information such as date of birth; the individual's position in the family; and any change since the last census in the status of family members, such as marriage and adoption, is recorded in this register. The census register refers to the married couple. When a couple is married, they apply to the Municipal Council for a new entry to be made. Normally, they apply to the Council where the husband's side of the family is registered, but in theory a couple may choose to be registered in another area. They can also transfer the registered address elsewhere at a later date.

Date of Birth

When giving one's year of birth, the year of the imperial rule is often given, rather than the year according to the Gregorian calendar. The year in which a new emperor ascends the throne is counted as the first year of a period, and this period is given a name or title. The present Emperor came to power in 1989, so the birthday of a child born on the 22nd of November, 1990, would be written as:

Upon the death of the late Showa Emperor (Hirohito), Japan named the new era **Heisei**, 平成, which means 'Completed Peace'. It replaced **Showa**, 昭和, the name of Emperor Hirohito's reign, which meant 'Enlightened Peace'. The name of a period, **nengoo**, is usually chosen from the Chinese classics by an academic committee.

Notice also that in writing dates, the year precedes the month which precedes the day. This is so whether imperial reign dates or the Gregorian calendar are used.

Age

A person's age is socially a very important concern for Japanese. There are expectations attached to age, relating to appropriate attitudes, thinking, and marital and social status. The tendency to be concerned about age is probably related to the need to maintain 'face' or **sekentei**. Social norms and expectations associated with age are closely adhered to. (See chapter 7, *The Importance of Age*.)

Most Japanese would share a belief in a social timetable which links specific achievements to ages appropriate for their attainment. For example, persons who plan to undertake tertiary education begin immediately upon graduation from high school, provided they have passed the appropriate entrance examinations. This is unlike countries such as Australia, where many people start further education after having worked for several years. It is extremely rare to see older students in Japan. In fact, a typical reaction to a person starting university in their thirties, for example, would be, 'What for, at your age?'.

As a working member of society, a person, especially a man, is expected to attain certain positions at certain ages, such as becoming a manager at forty.

Marriage is also related to age. There is even a word, **tekireiki**, which refers to the most suitable age for marriage. Although life in Japan has become more diverse, with the **tekireiki** now later than it was, the social expectation still remains that there is a suitable age at which people should marry. Recent statistics show that the average age at present for marriage is twenty-six for women and twenty-nine for men.

The general attitude with regard to age and its relation to appropriate behaviour is illustrated in common expressions such as **toshigai mo nai**, 'not acting one's age', and **ii toshi o shite**, 'old enough to know not to ...'.

Publicly, age is also a matter of interest to Japanese. In newspapers and magazines it is common practice to mention the age of a person, usually by putting it in parentheses after the name: 'Kazuko Yoshiyama (28), is a ...'.

Occupation

When asked about their occupation, most Japanese give an answer such as, 'I work for a computer-related company', or 'I am a company employee'. This is partly because a person's 'belonging' to a particular company takes precedence over their actual occupation. In fact, most companies do not employ a person as a specialist for a specific position. Rather, staff are all regarded as members of the company. The demarcation of specific positions and the boundaries between particular jobs is not as clearly drawn as in Australia.

The sense of belonging tends to be related to the length of service in a particular company. About 30 per cent of the Japanese workforce enjoy lifetime employment, and among these employees, the sense of commitment to their company is very strong.

Another reason for not specifying position may be modesty. When people, especially people engaged in highly regarded positions, are asked about their actual work, they usually reply vaguely, saying, for example that their work is 'law-related'.

As well as the traditional outlook on work, changing values are also evident, especially among the young. Many of the new generation prefer to change jobs in order to obtain greater job satisfaction than would be possible if they stayed with the same company. This tendency is particularly strong among women, as companies in general remain conservative and do not give women many opportunities for advancement. The word **torabaayu**, from the French travail meaning 'work', means 'to change jobs', and is often used to illustrate the dissatisfaction many women feel with their present status in the workplace. **Torabaayu** is also the title of a magazine in which job vacancies are advertised.

As well as the challenge to the 'single company' concept, the concept of 'belonging' is also being rejected. Some young people take a number of casual jobs in order to save for the future or get enough money to realise their dreams, such as opening their own business or going on a world trip.

Ethnicity

The statement made in a public speech by one of Japan's politicians, that Japan is ethnically homogenous, proved to be extremely controversial. Strong protests were received from several Japanese ethnic groups and a public apology was required.

The statement itself was not exceptional. If asked about ethnicity, many Japanese would reply in exactly the same manner. There is in fact a lack of awareness, even naivety, about ethnic issues.

There are over 700 000 Koreans living in Japan. The majority of them were brought to Japan during the period when Japan occupied Korea from 1910-45. Although the Korean community still maintains its own identity, the younger generation rarely learn the Korean language.

The second major ethnic group after the Koreans is the Ainu, native Japanese whose forebears were driven to the northern island of Hokkaido by the Yamato, forebears of the majority of Japanese today. The Ainu comprise a very small percentage of the population and the Ainu language is on the verge of extinction. A revival of Ainu identity is urgently needed.

Ethnic Chinese form a third minority group, a group which principally resides within specific Chinese districts.

As for the Yamato people, that is, the vast majority of the Japanese people, their origin is unclear. Some anthropologists believe they came from Mongolia and reached the Japanese archipelago via the Korean peninsula. Others believe that they were originally a rice-growing culture from the South Asian region. Among the Yamoto Japanese, one group, the **burakumin**, should not be neglected, although they are not a separate ethnic group *per se*. During the Edo period, when the Tokugawa shogunate divided society into four classes, there were those who did not fall into any clear category. Among these were leather workers, weapon makers, executioners, sufferers from chronic diseases such as leprosy, vagrants and others. Under the influence of Buddhism, which forbids the killing of living things, such people were regarded as impure and labelled as 'untouchable'. In other cases, the Tokugawa shogunate deprived certain groups of artisans of social status in order in establish a monopoly of special skills. In 1871, when the Meiji emperor abolished the class system, the **burakumin** were in theory also emancipated. Nevertheless, injustice continues in the form of discrimination in spite of countermeasures enacted by the government.

At present, **burakumin** and other minority ethnic groups in Japan are generally disadvantaged. Marriage, employment and other social opportunities are all hindered because of prejudice, resulting mainly from the lack of awareness of those who believe in the myth of Japan's ethnic homegeneity.

Classroom Tasks

■ Task 1 ■

Australians and Japanese write their addresses in quite different ways. Imagine you work in the post office and have been asked to write a pamphlet explaining how to address an envelope in Australia.

Design the pamphlet. Don't forget to explain:

- ■ How and where to write the receiver's address
- ■ How and where to write the sender's address
- ■ Where to put the stamp!

■ Task 2 ■

Below are two copies of an embarkation card. How would the following Japanese fill in the 'occupation' section of the card?

Name	Family Name	Given Name
Date of Birth		
Address		
Occupation		

a) Mr Kooji Shimada, in charge of the accounting section at Mitsutomo Bank

b) Miss Toshiko Matsui, a secretary at Kakuta Trading Company

c) Mr Yukio Tanaka, a school teacher working at a public school

How would the following Australians fill in the card?

Name	Family Name	Given Name
Date of Birth		
Address		
Occupation		

d) Mr John Carter, a school teacher working at a public school

e) Ms Pauline Jamieson, a shop assistant in Grace Brothers Department store

f) Ms Sally Atkinson, an architect with Smith, Brown and Company

Are there any differences in the way people from the two cultures fill in the card?

What do you think the differences tell you about people's attitude to employment in each country?

Task 3

Australia is a multicultural society. What does this mean?

- In pairs, write a definition of a 'multicultural society', then compare your definition with the definition given in the Macquarie Dictionary.
- What aspects of daily life do you think reflect multiculturalism most clearly?
- What advantages do you think multiculturalism has given Australia?
- How do you think Australia might improve its multiculturalism?
- Do you think multiculturalism has resulted in any problems for Australia?

Terms of Address

When arriving for the first time in Australia, Japanese often remark on the informality of many aspects of life. Using first names in public situations, such as in the office, is a case in point.

Hierarchy and Terms of Address

As mentioned above, use of first names is felt to be strange, particularly when differences in status or age are concerned. A Japanese student studying in an Australian university expressed her feelings like this: 'I can never get used to the idea of calling my lecturers Michael, or Helen or Tony. I have to take a great gulp before saying it. I don't know why, but I feel that by using their first names, I am deviating from the social distance I should keep from them.'

This comment is understandable in the light of Japanese customs regarding terms of address, which differ markedly from Australian ones. Of several differences, the most distinctive is that in Japanese it is considered rude to call an older person or a person of higher status by their first name. This may be the reason why Japanese students in Australia tend to say 'excuse me' rather than use the teacher's name when attracting attention.

Look at the dialogue below:

Kojima: Manager, the document from the XYZ Company has arrived.

Yoshida: OK. Then let's have a meeting about it this afternoon. Kojima-***kun***, please let everyone know.

Kojima, being junior in position, employs Yoshida's title when addressing him. Yoshida however calls Kojima by his actual surname as Kojima is a subordinate.

The custom of avoiding using a person's name goes back to the court culture of ancient Japan, when the names of the nobility were regarded as a reflection of their souls. It was therefore sacrilegious to utter them. Names are, of course, no longer considered to be sacred, but the custom of avoiding their use has continued.

Suffixes

In this section, we will explore how people address each other in everyday life, paying special attention to how differences in status are reflected in the way people address others in their social network.

Deference when addressing a person of higher status is expressed by avoiding the use of their actual name. In the classroom, for example, students call their teacher ***sensei***, 'teacher' or 'master', or ***Tanaka sensei***, 'Teacher Tanaka', in which the title is accompanied by the family name. The term ***sensei*** is often employed as a general term to refer to a person of higher status – a teacher, a doctor or even a politician.

Apart from the use of titles, suffixes can be attached to a person's name, forming the equivalent of the English Mr, Mrs and Miss.

In the spoken language, -**san** is a general suffix which is used regardless of sex and marital status. It can be added to either the family name or the first name, the former conveying a sense of greater formality:

Johnson-**san**

Ono-**san**

As well as -**san**, -**kun** and -**chan** can also be used. -**Kun** is usually used when addressing people of equal or lower status. It has a slight feeling of intimacy, and expresses the warm and friendly feeling of an elder to a younger person. Boys in primary and secondary school are often addressed as -**kun**, while girls are called -**san**. In each case, the suffix is attached to the family name. In the office, junior staff regardless of sex are often addressed using -**kun**.

Chan is a suffix that expresses intimacy. It is generally used when addressing children or people with whom the speaker is on intimate terms, especially if that person is younger.

It should also be noted that suffixes tend not to be used between people whose relationship is very close, such as couples or close friends. Such people call each other by first name or nickname.

Having examined how Japanese address each other, we will now take an individual case and see how these terms are used in an actual social network.

Naoko is a high school history teacher. She is twenty-eight years old and lives with her parents in a small suburb of Tokyo where she was born and brought up.

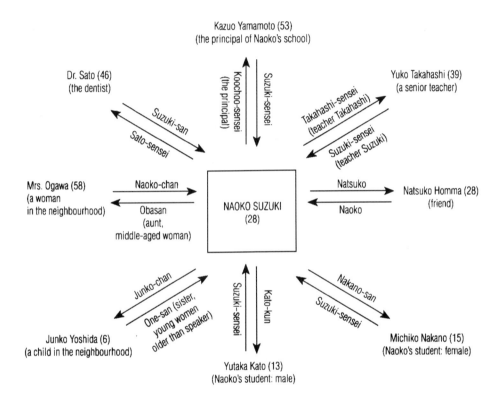

Naoko's Social Network

(ages indicated in brackets)

> Why do you think that Australians tend to stress the use of first names?
>
> How do you feel when addressed by your title and family name?
>
> How would you explain Australian attitudes to naming to your Japanese students?

Classroom Task

Look at the diagram below. It explains how Naoko Suzuki, a teacher in a Japanese school, addresses different people.

Draw up a similar diagram and ask your teacher how she addresses similar people in Australia and how they address her.

When you have filled in the Australian diagram, compare the two.

What differences do you find in the way people address each other?

What does this tell you about the differences between life in Japan and life in Australia?

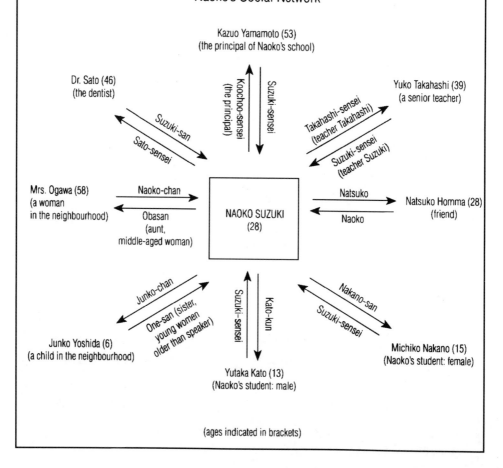

Family Relationships

The Japanese Family Today

Traditionally, the Japanese have enjoyed an extended family system whereby several generations lived under the same roof. The eldest couple, particularly the husband, was financially dominant under the patriarchal system of the pre-war constitution. The eldest son would succeed him as patriarch or head of the family.

Nowadays, the majority of Japanese families are nuclear families. In many cases, however, the eldest son remains within the family household after marriage. He and his wife begin to assume the responsibilities of the head of the family as his parents gradually withdraw from the active handling of family affairs. Other children leave the family home after marriage. They embark on new lives, forming a new nuclear family if they are males, or marrying into a different family if they are females.

During the last decade, an increasing number of young couples, particularly in urban areas, have come to resent the idea of living with their parents. Nevertheless, factors such as the housing shortage, steep increases in land prices, the ageing society and changes in career consciousness among women have all tended to increase the attractiveness of co-residence. One recent trend is for the family to build an extension onto the main house, which allows both the young couple and their parents to live independent lives on the same premises.

Even though nowadays some couples initially live apart from their parents, it is taken for granted that one couple, usually the eldest son and his wife, will look after the ageing parents. The idea of old people finishing their lives in nursing homes is unacceptable and young couples who place their parents in such homes are considered by most people to be irresponsible. It is of course true that nursing homes do exist and that circumstances such as shortage of living space or incompatibility between, for example, the mother-in-law and the daughter-in-law, result in some old people being placed in them. This is very definitely considered undesirable.

The Family and the Individual

The role of each individual in a Japanese marriage is often misinterpreted by overseas visitors. Having briefly observed the Japanese family, they comment on the dominance of men over women. The picture of the wife working in the kitchen while her husband sits at the table calling for tea and the newspaper, or the woman's seemingly reserved demeanour, give the impression that women are oppressed.

However, this impression is based on behaviour in front of guests. Many people feel it is appropriate to adopt traditional roles in public, irrespective of their actual roles at home. Presentation of what is considered to be a harmonious image is very important for 'face'.

Despite Western misconceptions, men today, especially young men, don't play a particularly chauvinistic role in the family. In fact, husband and wife usually have an equal say in household decisions such as the education of their children.

In most cases, the wife is in charge of the household budget. The husband usually hands over his entire salary packet to his wife and receives an allowance. Roles and responsibilities within the family are clearly demarcated, with the women expected to take care of the housework while the men engage in work outside the home. As men, especially company employees, devote long hours to work, total responsibility for household affairs usually devolves on the woman. In spite of an increasing number of married women who wish to continue their careers, most women still leave work after child-birth. This is partly due to the general inflexibility of working conditions and partly due to the traditional idea that child-rearing is a woman's most important task.

In most Japanese families, children are the paramount concern. The child's success, especially in education, is valued very highly and parents try to provide the very best education possible, even to the extent of considerable self-sacrifice. This is particularly true for the families of company employees. When a husband is transferred to another office for a period, often several years, the wife usually does not accompany him to his new post lest the children's education be adversely affected. A large percentage of the household budget is spent on education. This includes fees for the *juku*, private institutions which provide additional hours of classroom education to prepare children for school and university entrance examinations.

In order to enter a school with high academic standards, children start *juku* as early as fourth or fifth grade. Such primary school children would attend *juku* two or three times a week, coming home as late as seven o'clock in the evening. After the evening meal, they retire to their bedrooms to do their homework. Children's rooms are called 'studies', **benkyoo-beya**, rather than bedrooms. A desk is normally bought for each child as soon as he or she starts school. Parents try to provide their children with the best possible study environment, even if their accommodation situation is not particularly good. Partly because of these high expectations to do well at school, students are usually excused from household chores.

Children are usually financially supported by their parents until their tertiary education is completed. Although many university students take part-time jobs, this is mostly to earn extra pocket money. The school rules of many secondary schools forbid the taking of part-time jobs as it is considered that such jobs expose children to temptations which may lead to juvenile delinquency. There is thus a tendency to shield children from 'the real world'.

Parental supervision extends until children get married. A person is not considered to be fully independent while they are single. Unmarried children are normally expected to live with their parents except in cases where children have to attend a university far from the family home. Once children start working, they usually pay their parents board to cover part of the food expenses.

People are normally expected to consult their parents for guidance on a marriage partner. Although they choose their own marriage partners, it is important that the parents consent. A person does not therefore simply announce their engagement but seeks approval for it. From the parents' viewpoint, child-rearing is finally complete when and only when, all their children are married.

Terms for Family Relationships

Japanese distinguishes between elder and younger brothers and sisters:

	Elder	Younger
brother	onii-san	otooto
sister	onee-san	imooto

Names are avoided when addressing senior members of the family. When a younger brother addresses an older brother, for example, **onii-san**, 'elder brother' is used. The elder brother would however use his younger brother's given name when addressing him.

Once a child is born, the couple tend to call each other **otoo-san**, 'father', and **okaa-san**, 'mother'. This reflects the defined roles of the couple in the family.

The following chart demonstrates the terms of address used in the Yamamoto family. The family consists of Mr and Mrs Yamamoto, Yone (Mr Yamamoto's mother) and three children.

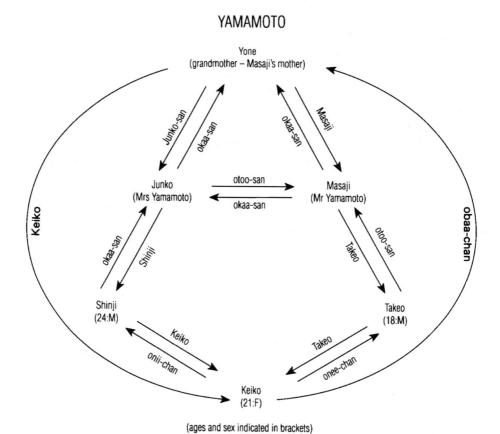

(ages and sex indicated in brackets)

When talking about family members with people outside the family, a different set of terms is used, a set that is more humble than the honorific terms used when addressing a person directly.

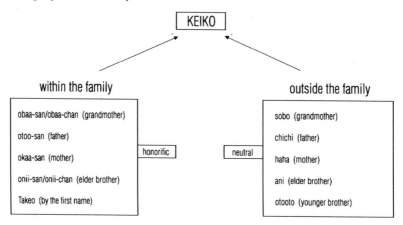

Classroom Tasks

■ Task 1 ■

Draw up your own family tree and show how you address each member of your family.

Ask an Australian — a friend or your teacher — about his or her family tree. Draw the tree and write in how the members of an Australian family address each other.

What similarities and what differences do you find?

■ Task 2 ■

In pairs, answer the following questions about Japanese family life. Then ask the same questions of an Australian, a friend or work-mate, or your teacher:

a) Who is the head of the household?

b) Who runs the household?

c) Who does the housework? Is it shared between family members? If so, how is it shared?

d) What responsibilities do children have around the home?

e) When do the children finally leave home?

f) Where do the grandparents live?

Compare your answers with the answers of other students in the class. What do they tell you about similarities and differences in family life in Australia and Japan?

Have your ideas about Australian family life changed since you came to Australia? If so, how?

Friendship

For many Japanese, friendship is based on being part of a small group that remains friends for a long time. Friendships are usually forged at school or university, or at work. Many university students form groups based around the activities of particular clubs, and they organise their schedules around those activities. The sense of belonging to the same group provides the foundation of friendship and defines the identity of each person involved.

Once someone joins a group, they do not normally move from that group to another. Persons are expected to commit themselves and in return receive unlimited support from the group. In this respect, many Japanese express disappointment in dealing with Australian friends, finding Australian friendships to be very distant. When individual interests take precedence over a person's commitment to the group, or when a person occasionally associates with different groups of friends to do different things, Japanese tend to feel that that person is not fulfilling the obligations of friendship.

Australians place a high priority on privacy and the rights of the individual. Also, friends remain friends even after long absences. Japanese, on the other hand, tend to reaffirm friendship constantly by being with each other all the time.

An Australian living in Japan as an exchange student reported that at first she enjoyed the intimacy and constant contact that was involved in Japanese friendships, but that she gradually began feeling that she had lost her privacy, as she had to spend so much time with the same group of people. She commented, 'Japanese friends seem to live in each other's pockets all the time.'

Another characteristic of Japanese friendship is the limited opportunities available to meet other people. Friendships are usually formed within a person's immediate environment, such as the school or the company. There are few social gatherings, such as parties, where a person has the opportunity to meet new people. Hence, social networks tend to be different and more limited than they are in Australia.

> Yoshiko Yamada was in Australia visiting Jenny Watson. Jenny had stayed with Yoshiko's family in Japan as an exchange student. Having observed Jenny's way of relating to her friends, Yoshiko felt that her friendships were very shallow. When one of her friends rang to ask her out to dinner, Jenny refused, saying, 'Sorry, I really am exhausted today. Do you mind if I give it a miss?' Yoshiko wondered why Jenny didn't make an effort to respond more positively to her friend and felt Jenny was just being selfish.
>
> Is Yoshiko right in her interpretation of Jenny's behaviour?
>
> How would you explain the Australian idea of friendship and its obligations to her?

Leisure Activities

The Japanese activity **karaoke** has spread to many countries and is widely accepted today. **Karaoke** is generally found in bars and restaurants, and consists of a selection of popular songs on video. The customer selects the song to be played and sings along with it from a stage, microphone in hand, for the entertainment or otherwise of the other patrons of the bar. The idea is that **karaoke** is an extra attraction when going out for a drink. It suits the Japanese lifestyle, since many people drop into bars with colleagues after spending long hours at work.

Similarly, many leisure activities revolve around a person's workplace and involve friends made at work or at university. In fact, some companies offer clubs, such as tennis clubs and baseball clubs, and recreational facilities such as holiday houses to their staff. It is also common practice for employers to organise a group tour once a year so that staff members, irrespective of status, can spend time together and strengthen group harmony. Families of staff are sometimes included in these types of activities.

Weekend activities have diversified as an increasing number of employers have now granted a two-day weekend. Many businessmen play golf with their colleagues at the weekend, particularly in order to entertain their clients, so it is important for businessmen to learn how to play. Japanese are also keen participants in various other sports. Tennis, hiking, baseball and skiing are popular with all age groups.

Shopping is a very popular leisure activity. Many people go shopping in their leisure time because they have no time to do so during the week. At the same time, shopping offers more than the mere act of buying. Some department stores, for example, offer cultural facilities such as art galleries, lecture halls, cinemas and concert halls so that people can combine shopping with other entertainment.

Coffee shops are very popular meeting points, especially among young people, who often meet in a coffee shop rather than at home. From there, they may go on to a movie or shopping, or they may also just sit and chat. Pop music is as widespread in Japan as it is in Australia, and both Japanese and foreign bands can be heard. Television is obviously popular with all age groups and many households have two or more television sets. Video rental shops are common and rental rates are comparable with those in Australia.

Young unmarried men with high disposable incomes often lavish a lot of attention on their cars, an interest that they share with Australian men!

> Many foreign students find it difficult to make Australian friends and claim that Australians are rather 'closed'.
>
> Why do you think they might feel this?
>
> Do you think there is any way of overcoming this impression?

Classroom Tasks

■ Task 1 ■

How did you meet your three best friends? And where did you meet them? How long have you known them?

Ask two other Japanese the same questions.

Then ask three Australians.

Report your findings to the rest of the class.

What are the similarities and what are the differences in the way that Australians and Japanese make friends?

■ Task 2 ■

Catherine, an Australian living in Japan, had this to say about her Japanese friends:

When I first arrived, of course I didn't know anyone, but I quickly made friends and it was great. We went everywhere together and saw each other constantly. However, after a while I noticed that I wasn't meeting anyone new, it was always the same group of people. And I never seemed to have any time to myself. It seemed that we were all living in one anothers' pockets.

Why do you think Catherine felt like this?

Meeting People and Making Casual Conversation

When meeting someone for the first time, Japanese people tend to ask personal questions such as a person's age and occupation. It is rare to have a discussion on social issues. This is because Japanese tend to feel it is important to pass through several phases before they can talk freely about many issues. The first step in getting to know someone is to make clear who a person is and how they fit into the overall framework of society. Questions on age and occupation are important in establishing this. Non-personal topics of conversation, such as the exchange of opinions, come later as the relationship deepens.

Japanese are generally not used to carrying out a conversation merely for the sake of being social. They are often surprised to see strangers in public places such as in supermarkets or on trains exchanging casual conversation. If they see people in a queue talking about a general topic such as the cricket, they would usually assume that the people knew each other. The following incident illustrates this attitude. Mr and Mrs Hayashi were invited to a social tennis match. At the tennis court they were greeted in a friendly manner. The conversation ran on general topics such as real estate prices, a new car model that one of the players had heard about and the current political and economic climate. When the Hayashis learned that all the people there that day had just met for the first time, they were shocked that such a lively conversation about general topics had been going on. They felt that several stages in the relationship had been skipped to have reached this stage of intimacy.

Japanese students at language schools and universities also express similar feelings. Australian students and other students from Europe start talking about subjects of mutual interest from the beginning of their friendship. If they are interested in films, they start talking about films without knowing anything about each other.

Many Japanese are hesitant to interact closely with someone until they know more about the person they are talking to. Japanese need to feel that their relationships with others go through a developmental stage. This reluctance to talk about general topics early in an acquaintance often causes Japanese to feel uncomfortable when meeting people from other cultures. Teachers should remember that their Japanese students need to develop skills in this area as such skills are important in the formation of friendships.

> What do you talk about when you meet someone for the first time, say at a party?
>
> Are there any topics you would feel uncomfortable talking about?
>
> Do the materials you use in teaching examine the sort of topics that are discussed when people meet each other for the first time? Or are these topics taken for granted?
>
> How would you supplement your teaching material to ensure that Japanese students were familiar with Australian usage?

Classroom Task

What do people talk about in casual conversation?

Over the next week, try and note down what kind of topics people talk about in everyday conversation. Listen to people on the bus or train, at work, having a cup of coffee, etc.

Make a copy of the chart on next page and note down your observations and your reactions. One has been done for you to get you started.

Where	Who	Topic of Conversation	Comments
Supermarket queue	two women	Things they were buying	Women seemed to be strangers. In Japan, we don't usually talk to strangers.

Male-Female Relationships

Many Australians believe that Japanese women are subservient to men. Such an image is not necessarily true in modern Japan, though it is true that Japanese women are still given limited opportunities to pursue careers. The age-old division of labour is yet to change. On a personal level, however, women are not dominated by men. In particular, both partners in a marriage have an equal say in any decisions to be made.

Having said this, it is important to stress that social conventions dictate what are masculine roles and what are feminine. Both men and women feel that, in public, it is appropriate to act in accordance with such conventions. On social occasions, for example, men normally initiate the conversation and guide the development of the subject. Women are generally expected to listen. It would in fact be seen as aggressive if a woman spoke as much as a man in conversation. When in a country like Australia, some Japanese men confess that they feel a little intimidated, if not offended, by women being equally involved in an exchange of opinions in either a casual social setting such as a party, or at the office.

Japanese are generally conscious of how they appear in society. At present, Japanese society expects specific standards of behaviour and values the maintenance of these standards. Many Japanese feel it appropriate to conform, at least in public. In a personal relationship, however, there is no consciousness that male chauvinism is oppressing the female. For example, when a Japanese couple attend a social gathering, the wife tends to take a subservient role, walking a step behind her husband, nodding her head at whatever he says as if she is in total agreement. Although the Japanese wife may appear to be the victim of male chauvinist attitudes, neither she nor her husband would usually agree with this interpretation. They would consider that they were acting appropriately and in accordance with legitimate social norms. Such behaviour is not considered to be indicative of lack of equality. Women are seen as having responsibilities that are different from, but of equal value to, those of men. Couples tend to feel that in their private relationship, each respects the other's position and opinions and each has an equal say in family decisions.

Because of the prevailing expectations regarding male and female roles, it is difficult to have egalitarian platonic friendships. Deviation from conventional roles is not generally accepted. It may be for this reason that male and female students tend to sit separately in the classroom.

Another misconception about male-female relationships concerns marriage. Many foreigners believe that arranged marriages (in the strict sense, where the free will of the individual is ignored), are still practised in Japan. According to recent statistics, however, more than 70 per cent of marriages are 'love-matches' as opposed to *o-miai* or arranged marriages.

An *o-miai* is a meeting arranged by a go-between. Before the man and the woman actually meet, photographs, curricula vitae and other personal information are exchanged. A refusal can easily be given if one party does not like the other. In this respect, the *o-miai* is a pragmatic practice which offers young men and women opportunities to meet the ideal (in a practical sense) marriage partner.

As we have seen, the typical image of Japanese male-female relationships is rather inaccurate. Although women are still disadvantaged at work or are indifferent to the prospect of a career — an indifference that is mainly due to the common idea that marriage and child-rearing constitute a woman's supreme achievement — Japanese men and women today maintain an egalitarian relationship, particularly in private.

> When observing Japanese male-female relationships, many Australians are biased by their own cultural conceptions of appropriate behaviour.
>
> What behaviour and attitudes regarding male-female relationships are considered appropriate in Australia?
>
> How would you introduce such behaviour and attitudes to your Japanese students?

Classroom Task

In this task, we will examine how household duties are shared between husband and wife.

Ask four Australians and four Japanese who usually does the housework in their families and fill in the details on the chart on next page. Use W if the wife is responsible and H if the husband is responsible.

Duty	Australian				Japanese			
Occupation husband wife								
Cooking								
Washing up								
Setting table								
Cleaning:								
kitchen								
bedroom								
bathroom								
toilet								
Laundry								
Ironing								
Shopping								
Gardening								
Taking out rubbish								
Washing car								
Household finances								

CHAPTER ■ FIVE

LIVING IN SOCIETY

In the following chapter, we will look at various aspects of everyday life in Japan.

Employment

Every autumn, when recruitment of new graduates and school leavers begins, major cities in Japan are flooded with students hunting for a job. Wearing suits for the first time, they run from one interview to another. The season represents judgment day for many students, as their whole lives may be determined during this period.

In Japan, lifetime employment is commonly practised by large companies. While people working in small companies and those working for sub-contractors do not in general enjoy the advantages conferred by the large companies, there is a general expectation that employees will in fact remain more or less permanently in the same job. Australian expectations of job mobility are not shared by Japanese.

Unlike many Western countries where companies employ people whose skills can be effective immediately, Japanese companies select applicants with potential who can be trained to become suitable employees. For this reason, recruiting employees is an important exercise for companies, as they invest a lot of time and money in training new staff. This is basically true both for factory workers and for professionals. Professionals who have studied subjects which are of immediate use in the workplace, such as industrial engineers, are very often placed in factories and transferred from one section to another. By gaining experience in several different areas and by working in close contact with workers, the engineers are believed, in the long run, to become more effective members of the company. Workers too feel more involved by working with professionals and by being allowed to voice their opinions. Loyalty is believed to be cultivated in this type of egalitarian working environment.

Because of this system of training employees to be all-rounders, mobility between companies is low. Wages are set according to educational background or initial field of employment, ordinary graduates being employed in administration, engineers in engineering and design departments and so on. Both promotions and wage increases tend to be tied to seniority, though some differences may arise later on as a result of ability and business performance. Wages are paid monthly, and the net sum, after the deduction of tax, is usually paid directly into a bank account. As well as salary, a bonus is usually paid twice a year. This is a custom that dates back to the time when employers gave special allowances so that employees could properly celebrate **bon**, a Buddhist festival held in mid-July in Tokyo, but on other dates in other regions. The festival is held to appease the souls of ancestors. The second bonus is distributed at New Year. Recently, bonuses have also been offered as a way of allowing workers a share in the profits that their hard work has gained.

A large number of people go through the kind of employment process described above. Some professions, however, recruit in a different manner. School teachers wishing to teach in the public schools must pass an examination administered by each prefecture's board of education which also sets the wages.

Many female graduates complain that they are not given equal training and equal opportunity in comparison to male graduates. Japanese companies generally believe that female employees will eventually leave to get married and have children. It is also true that, as well as the still-existing belief among women themselves that nothing should stand in the way of child-rearing, the extended hours of work often do not allow women to continue their careers after marriage.

Disappointed career-minded female graduates often opt to work for foreign firms. Since most male graduates prefer to join Japanese firms with their guaranteed security, foreign firms are often keen to employ female graduates as their potential tends to be greater than that of male applicants.

Some men, however, do leave their companies in spite of future prospects, one reason being to take over the family business. The eldest sons in families that own family companies or businesses such as stores are normally expected to take over the business when their parents retire. It is therefore quite common to see a businessman, on succeeding to his parents' business, completely change his professional direction by becoming, for example, a shop keeper.

In other cases, employees quit because of conflicts between the duties involved in their work and their desire for a particular lifestyle. Young workers, particularly, may change jobs to find more fulfilling ones. Companies are prepared to recruit such young people, as they believe they can be retrained to suit their needs.

On the job, working relationships tend to be very close because of the long hours of work and years of service in common. Social life in fact is frequently based on the workplace. Restaurants and **nomi-ya**, 'pubs', are always crowded at night with people enjoying an evening out with their colleagues. Many companies also organise trips and sports days for their employees.

Senior staff often play the role of mentor. This involves becoming involved in the lives of junior staff in such things as marriage and the children's education.

The average age of retirement is between 55 and 60. For most Australians, retirement may be an eagerly awaited time to undertake such things as travel and hobbies. Many Japanese, however, simply cannot get used to the freedom of retirement and they look for ways of constructively using their time. Many look for new jobs, feeling that if they do not work they will be abandoned by society. This has recently led to the development in some municipalities of municipal job centres which advertise casual work such as cleaning and lawn mowing. Given that Japan is facing the problem of an increasingly ageing society, such activities may be vital in the future.

Classroom Tasks:

■ Task 1 ■

Compare the following Australian and Japanese job advertisements:

i) What kind of employees are they looking for?

ii) What does each advertisement stress in order to attract applicants?

Sales Representative

Are you:

- ☞ *Qualified in biochemistry/microbiology?*
- ☞ *Independent and outgoing?*
- ☞ *Seeking a rewarding and challenging career?*

If you answer YES to all of the above, you may be just the right person to join in our NSW sales team.

A competitive salary package will be negotiated with the successful candidate.

If this sounds like You, please reply in writing, marked 'confidential' to:

**Hightech Biological Services,
PO Box 1111, Newville, NSW 2222.**

We, a leading company in software design, are looking for enthusiastic staff.

SALES STAFF

Qualifications: 22-29 years of age

University Degree

Salary: Based on age and experience

Conditions:
- salary rise once a year
- bonus — twice a year
- transport allowance provided
- social insurance provided
- men's dormitory available
- recreational facilities

Send your curriculum vitae with a photograph to:

**Fujisawa Co. Ltd
Aoki Bldg. 4F
4 - 3 - 5 Jingu-mae
Shibuya-ku Tokyo**

■ Task 2 ■

Below are some terms that are important im enployment in Japan. Explain each of these terms to your teacher.

■ What do they mean and why are they important?

■ Are these ideas important in Australia?

The first one is done for you.

i) ***Aotagai*** 青田買い

Aotagai literally means 'to buy rice before it is reaped.' In Japan, job-hunters start looking for jobs in autumn before they graduate the following March. An informal agreement, reached under the guidance of the Ministry of Labour, discourages companies from starting to recruit new graduates until a mutually agreed date. However, companies wanting to get the best employees may unofficially contact graduates and conduct interviews before this date. This is called aotagai.

ii)	rikuruuto suutsu	リクルートスーツ	– a recruitee's suit
iii)	nenkoo joretsu	年功序列	– the seniority system
iv)	boonasu	ボーナス	– a bonus
v)	kootsuuhi shikyuu	交通費支給	– a commuting allowance

When you have explained these terms, find out what the following five Australian terms mean:

i) Perks

ii) Holiday loading

iii) Double time

iv) Flexi-day

v) A long weekend

■ Task 3 ■

Below are examples of job application forms from Japan and Australia. What kind of information is the employer looking for in each case? How does each form reflect the employment system of the country concerned?

履歴書						
氏名 name		印 seal	性別 sex	写真 photo	特技 special skills	
現住所 present address			電話: phone		得意な科目 strong subjects	
本籍 registered address					趣味 personal interests	
					長所 personality : strong points	
履歴 personal history					短所 personality : weak points	
					応募の動機 a reason for application	
					家族構成 family information	
					氏名 name	職業 occupation	本人との続柄 relation to the applicant

EMPLOYMENT APPLICATION

Name: _____ Date of Birth: _____
      Family Name   First Name(s)

Address: _____ Telephone: _____
         _____
                   Postcode

Postal   _____
Address: _____
                   Postcode

Education:

Dates	School/University	Subjects	Qualifications

Employment History:

Employers' Name and Address	Position	Duties	Dates	Reason for Leaving

References:

Housing

Reflecting the continuing rise in land prices, more and more urban dwellers in Japan live in highrise apartment blocks, though there is also an increasing number of two to three storied houses being renovated. This is because, unable to afford a house of their own, married children are staying at home with their parents who rebuild the house in order to accommodate two or three generations beneath the same roof.

The average floor space of a Japanese home is a little less than 100 square metres, a figure which compares to the Australian average of 130 square metres and which is similar to that of several European countries.

At the moment, it is almost impossible for young couples to purchase a house in suburban areas. In fact, it is not until couples have been married for several years that they begin to consider buying a house. Single people have virtually no opportunity to do so. In Tokyo, the average price for an ordinary house is thirteen times the average family's annual income. Most couples therefore opt for a house or mansion — a euphemism for a highrise unit — in adjacent prefectures. Having decided on the purchase, people arrange a loan with the bank. The amount they can borrow is determined according to their annual income and the repayment period is approximately thirty years, though in some cases the obligation may be passed on to the next generation.

Young couples and single people would spend about one-third of their monthly income on rent. Unless living with their parents, most single young people live in flats or in company-supplied dormitories. These dormitories are provided for single men and for couples. However, women's dormitories are rare as companies think it more suitable for young women to commute from their parents' homes. Recently, economic difficulties have forced some companies to sell their dormitory buildings.

When a young couple or a single person decides to rent a flat, they first decide on the area in which they wish to live, taking into consideration factors such as distance to work, rent, and the size of available units, and then visit real estate agents.

```
            マンション　　　新築
          (mansion        recently built)
                  日当たり良
                  (sunny rooms)
              蕨駅より、徒歩１５分
         (15minutes walk from Warabi station)


             ２ＤＫ　（バス　トイレ付き）
   (with 2 bedrooms + dining place and kitchen + bath and toilet)
         家賃：　　８万円　＋　共益費　３、０００円
        (monthly rent 80,000 yen + maintenance fee 3,000 yen)
             礼金　　２か月分
         ( key money   for the owner - monthly rent× 2)
             敷金　　２か月分
         (bond  - monthly rent  ×  2)
```

As the advertisement shows, people tend to ask for newly built flats with sunny rooms. Distance to the station is an important consideration as most people are dependent on public transport to get to work. Real estate advertisements use symbols to describe the facilities offered. In this case, '2 DK' refers to two bedrooms, a **D**ining room and a **K**itchen.

As well as the monthly rent, a tenant also has to pay a monthly maintenance fee, a bond of two months' rent and finally key money, which might be described as a gift to the owner. Key money usually comprises two months' rent.

In most cases, rooms are completely unfurnished and tenants need to supply their own furniture, including stoves and refrigerators.

Unlike Australia, where shared accommodation is very common, the concept of living with strangers is foreign to most Japanese.

Describing a House

When Japanese come to Australia for the first time, they are often disappointed that many houses do not get a lot of sunshine. They also tend to dislike the fact that many houses are old. Japanese normally describe the ideal house as one that is 'bright, new and good', with the emphasis being placed on functional rather than aesthetic values. The practice of buying an old house and doing it up is not common in Japan.

In measuring rooms, the standard of the **tatami** mat is used. A **tatami** mat is a mat made of woven straw and is about 90 cm by 180 cm. An average room would be described as a six-mat room.

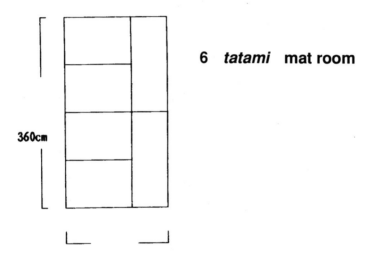

6 tatami mat room

An interesting feature of Japanese housing is that many houses have a guest room which is used for receiving and entertaining guests. Unlike the Australian family which gives its guests a tour of the house, Japanese expect their guests to remain in the guest room. They therefore often experience culture shock when invited to Australian houses. One Japanese couple reported that they had been invited to an Australian party and were surprised to see all the female guests gathered in the kitchen chatting with the hostess. Going beyond the guest room in someone else's house was to them unbelievable. This is particularly so with the kitchen, which in Japan is usually placed in the most undesirable part of the house, usually facing north, and is therefore the last place people are expected to gather.

With regard to undesirable parts of the house, it is interesting to note that the north is generally considered to be unfavourable as it is shaded and seldom gets direct sunlight.

As well as the guest room, the average Japanese house has a master bedroom, study-bedrooms for the children and a living room. Although lifestyles have been Westernised and there is a preference for Western furnishings such as beds and sofas rather than futons, that can be stored away when not in use, there is one custom that has not been modified. Most Japanese feel uncomfortable wearing shoes in the house. Even Japanese living in Australia say that it feels hard to relax with shoes on and it is also unhygienic. Many feel that their personal space is being violated. This is because the entrance, the place where shoes are taken off, marks the threshold separating outside from inside, and by extension, the public world from the private world.

> **In this section, we have examined some Japanese attitudes regarding guest access to various parts of the house.**
>
> **How do these attitudes compare with Australian attitudes to parts of the house?**
>
> **Do Australian attitudes vary with the occasion, e.g. party, barbeque, dinner party etc.?**
>
> **How would you introduce this aspect of social interaction to your class?**

Classroom Tasks

■ Task 1 ■

Draw a sketch of your home and answer the following questions about it:
i) What is each room used for?
ii) In which room does each member of the family spend most of his/her time?
iii) In which room would the following guests be entertained:
   * Relatives
   * Father's friends or colleagues
   * Mother's friends or colleagues
   * Children's friends

Now ask an Australian to sketch their house and ask them the same questions. What similarities and differences do you find?

■ Task 2 ■

Below is a comment made by Mr Carter, whose family is acting as host family to Takeshi, a Japanese exchange student. Based on your discussion in Task 1, how would you explain Takeshi's behaviour to the Carter's?

> Takeshi is a delightful boy and we enjoy having him as part of our family. He is very polite and makes a great effort at school. But there is one thing that we do not understand. In the evening after we finish our dinner, Takeshi goes straight to his room. He dosen't come out at all until he takes a shower before he goes to bed. I'm worried that he is homesick or that we've done something to upset him.

What advice would you give Takeshi to help him avoid this problem?

■ Task 3 ■

This task gives you an opportunity to investigate how Australian people live. Draw up a table like the one below and ask your Australian friends and teachers to help you fill it in. An example has been done for you.

Name	Occupation	Age	Housing Arrangements
Carol White	Hairdresser	24	Shares town house with one male, one female

How does the situation in Japan compare with the Australian situation? Explain the differences to your teacher.

Banking

Most Japanese have bank accounts and regard the provision of this service as the major function of a bank. There are two main types of accounts available to the general public, the ordinary account and the fixed-term account. An ordinary account allows people access to their money at any time and at any branch of the bank with which they have an account. Cash cards for use in automatic teller machines are widespread. A disadvantage of these ordinary accounts is the low rates of interest offered, usually about 1.5 per cent per annum. This means that most people open fixed-term accounts with money that is not required for immediate living expenses. These offer interest rates of about 3-5 per cent depending on the term chosen.

Accounts can also be opened at post offices. To open either a bank account or a post office account, personal identification such as a health insurance card or a driver's licence needs to be presented.

As in Australia, the use of credit cards has become widespread. Statistics show that more than 50 per cent of the population use them, mainly in shops and restaurants. Some expenses still cannot be paid by credit card: utility bills can only be paid by depositing the due sum directly into the account of the organisation in question. Cheques are not commonly used by individuals.

Service Encounters

Many Japanese find the casual attitude of Australian banking staff, particularly tellers, to be worrying. They tend to feel that too friendly an attitude reflects a lack of care in handling their money. An attitude of strict formality and absolute politeness is expected.

The explanation of this attitude lies in the importance in Japan of clear role differentiation. Unlike Australia, where the social value of egalitarianism extends to service encounters, customers in Japan expect to be received with a degree of deference. Mistakes caused by a customer's negligence would normally be covered up and correct procedures indirectly explained so as not to embarrass them. When a customer does not provide sufficient documentation, for example, the teller would first apologise for causing problems before requesting the correct documentation. A hierarchical relationship is maintained at all times.

A typical example of a service encounter, this one involving the payment of a bill, is reproduced below. The clerk throughout uses deferential language, while the customer is much more direct.

Acknowledgement
Teller: *irasshaimase*
'Welcome'

Request
Customer: *denwa ryookin no shiharai o shitai n desu ga*
'I would like to pay my telephone bill...'

Acceptance
Teller: *kashikomarimashita*
'Certainly'

Presentation of money and bill

(Customer presents incomplete form)
Apology and request
Teller: *mooshiwake gozaimasen*
'I am terribly sorry'
koko ni o-namae o onegai shimasu
'Would you mind writing your name here please'
Customer: *a hai kore de ii desu ka*
'Is this all right?'
Teller: *hai, sumimasen*
'Yes, thankyou'

Presentation
Teller: *o matase itashimashita*
'I am extremely sorry to have kept you waiting'
kochira wa o-kyaku-sama no hikae de gozaimasu
'This is your receipt'

Closing
Teller: *arigatoo gozaimashita*
'Thank you very much'
Customer: *doomo*
thanks

Shop assistants also tend to be more deferential than their Australian counterparts. Not only do shop assistants humbly address their customers, but body language is also used to express deference. Customers are often greeted at the entrance to department stores by young girls who bow in greeting. A browsing customer would immediately be approached by an assistant offering help and this assistant would then accompany the customer, pointing out various goods and giving relevant explanations until a satisfactory choice was made and the sale completed. Purchases are far more elaborately wrapped than would be the case in Australia.

> How is a service encounter, say in a department store, carried out in Australia?
>
> What impression do you think a newly arrived Japanese would gain of service in Australian shops and department stores?
>
> How would you help Japanese students correctly interpret the language and behaviour of Australian assistants?

Classroom Task

■ Task 1 ■

With a partner, go into an Australian department store.

While one of you buys something, the other should note down exactly what the shop assistant says.

Compare the way Australian shop assistants speak to their customers with the way Japanese shop assistants speak to theirs.

Imagine that a family friend, a women of about fifty, is going to visit Australia for the first time.

What would you tell her about Australian shop assistants?

■ Task 2 ■

In this task, you will conduct a small survey on Australian service and record your feelings about that service.

Draw up a chart with headings like the one below. When you go into a bank, shop, office or post-office during the next week, notice carefully how the tellers and assistants serve you. Record your observations on your form and add your comments. One has been given as an example.

When you have finished, compare your observations with those of others in your class. Then ask your Australian teacher for her comments. Do your evaluations agree? Why or why not?

Place	What was said/done	Your evaluation	Your teachers's evaluation
Bank	Teller: 'How are you?' 'Nice day, isn't it?'	Waste of time Unprofessional	Friendly, efficient service

Health

In Australia, a person who is sick usually goes first to a general practitioner and is then referred to a specialist if necessary. Japanese, on the other hand, choose their doctors according to the type of illness they are suffering from. They may consult their equivalent of our Yellow Pages in the local telephone directory or they may act on a personal recommendation. As in Australia, the doctor advertises his field of specialisation on a doorplate. Doctors may operate their own surgeries or clinics, or they may run small private hospitals offering several different areas of specialisation. Patients would normally go directly to such a private hospital for a consultation.

The Imai hospital in suburban Tokyo is owned by a couple, both of whom are doctors, one a surgeon and one a physician. The hospital accommodates twenty patients and has facilities such as an operating theatre and an X-ray machine. Patients consult the two doctors about problems ranging from colds to fractures and appendicitis. Apart from more serious cases, which need to be treated in larger hospitals such as those attached to universities, most people are treated in such small private hospitals. These hospitals also dispense medicines, so that a separate trip to the pharmacy is not necessary. When the couple retires, their son, at present studying medicine at university, will take over.

There is a general lack of interest in preventative medicine. Hospitals and clinics tend to be seen exclusively as concerned with curing rather than preventing. Nor do dentists particularly encourage people to have a six-monthly check-up as they do in Australia.

Traditionally, illness was considered to be related to the mental state of the individual. This attitude is reflected in the saying **yamai wa ki kara**, 病は気から 'illness comes from the mind'. Modern medical techniques have now almost entirely replaced traditional attitudes and the tendency nowadays is to emphasise local and specific rather than holistic treatment.

Medical insurance is normally arranged by the company for which a person works. Employees pay a monthly premium and this covers them for about 70 per cent of incurred medical expenses. For small businessmen and the self-employed, health cover is arranged by the local government under a national scheme.

One major difficulty experienced by many Japanese in dealing with Australian health services is the informality of communication between doctor and patient. In Japan, the relationship between doctor and patient is expected to be formal and hierarchic, and as such, there are no introductory comments such as greetings. All such non-medical conversation is left to the nurse who directs the patient to the doctor's office. It is also the nurse who explains to the patient how the medication prescribed by the doctor should be taken.

The doctor examines the patient and prescribes the appropriate treatment, but would not consider it appropriate to discuss either the illness or the treatment with the patient. The patient's role is entirely passive. In the case of serious illness, it is generally considered unacceptable to let the patient know the severity of his condition, which would rather be discussed with a family member.

The egalitarian approach adopted by most Australian doctors tends to make Japanese feel awkward and embarrassed. One Japanese student commented that she felt very uneasy when the doctor shook her hand, as to her handshaking belonged to a social and not to a professional setting.

How do you think you would react to the type of medical encounter described above?

How might you cope with such feelings

What could you suggest to your Japanese students who find themselves in a similar predicament in Australia?

Classroom Task

In Australia, where would you go if you had each of the following problems? And where would you go if you were in Japan?

i) You've got flu – a headache and a temperature.

ii) You've got a toothache.

iii) You've got a skin problem. Your skin is dry and itchy.

iv) You've got a bad earache.

v) You're playing football and you break your leg

vi) You're injured in a car accident.

What differences do you notice between the medical system in Australia and the medical system in Japan?

Getting Around

Public transport is the principal means of transport in Japan. In urban and suburban areas traffic is continually congested and the use of a car simply creates inconvenience and delay. Since trains and buses run every five minutes and more frequently during peak hours, public transport is quick and convenient.

This dependence on public transport influences the way in which Japanese describe distances. When asked how long it takes to get from one place to another, most people would reply that it takes 'about thirty minutes by train' or 'an hour by bus.' Descriptions given in terms of kilometres or miles often cause confusion.

The average Japanese spends one to two hours on the train every day. Commuting time is becoming longer every year because of the rise of property prices close to the city centres. This forces people to move further out in their search for affordable housing and some now face a two-hour commute each way.

People usually read books or newspapers while travelling. Comics are extremely popular, not only with children but with all sections of the community. All tastes are catered for, from martial arts and romance to history, economics and politics. The artistic standard of the graphics is often quite high. It is also common to see people asleep while seated. Public transport is in fact clean and safe and neither men nor women fear to travel on public transport even after midnight.

Most large companies pay for the commuting costs of their employees. Train passes are valid for one, three or six months and are purchased by individual employees who are then reimbursed by their company.

Although they are dependent on public transport during the week, many people are fond of using their cars during the weekend. Now that buying a house is becoming more and more of an impossible dream, some Japanese are opting to buy a car instead and there has been an increase in the number of people buying foreign luxury cars.

Japanese roads, unfortunately, are not well-designed for motor vehicles. They tend to be narrow and labyrinthine, making it a daunting task to look for a particular address. Many side streets are full of pedestrians and parking is often almost impossible to find, unless the driver is prepared to pay a carpark fee. Japanese traffic drives on the left.

For getting around the local community, such as going shopping, or getting to and from the station, bicycles are more convenient than cars. Many stations and shopping centres have parking areas for bicycles much as Australian stations and shopping centres have carparks.

Classroom Task

Different cultures give directions in different ways. Some talk about left and right and some use the compass directions (north, south, east and west); some use landmarks and some use maps.

Ask several Australians how to get to the nearest station. Which method do they use?

Do Japanese give directions in the same way? Explain to your teacher how Japanese give directions.

CHAPTER ■ SIX

INTERACTING IN SOCIETY

In this chapter, we will examine several aspects of social interaction. We are mainly interested in the interactive patterns that are essential for successful communication but which cannot be understood simply by applying linguistic knowledge. In other words, we are concerned with the social assumptions which underlie and shape people's utterances and which determine how we interpret them.

Greetings

Unlike greetings in English, which often employ the addressee's name as a sign of recognition and friendship, it is rare to use a personal name when greeting in Japanese. At the same time, calling someone by their title and family name sounds clumsy unless the person is addressed from a distance.

In a general setting such as on the street, a comment about the weather generally follows a greeting such as 'hello' or 'good morning'. Let's look at a conversation between neighbours:

Ishida:	*Konnichiwa*	
	Good afternoon	
Fukuda:	*Maa, konnichiwa*	
	Well, good afternoon	
Ishida:	*Zuibun atsuku narimashita ne*	
	It's getting very hot, isn't it?	
Fukuda:	*Hontoo ni*	
	Truly	

Another common expression used in greeting is **odekake desu ka**, 'Are you going out?' The speaker here is not actually interested in where the addressee is going and this is acknowledged in the expected vague response 'Yes, just over there.' It is in fact similar to the English greeting 'How are you', which is not a request for information about the speaker's state of health.

Greetings such as **ikaga desu ka**, which is similar in meaning to the English 'How are you?' and **o-genki desu ka**, 'Are you well?' were seldom used until recently. That they are now used more frequently may be due to the influence of English.

In informal settings, comments on a person's physical appearance may function as greetings. 'You have gained some weight, haven't you' is a common

Japanese greeting that is often taken as an insult by foreigners. One English teacher was upset when her Japanese student commented on a boil she had on her face. Her student was in fact only expressing his concern as part of the greeting ritual.

Greetings are very important. No matter how many times people run into each other during the course of a day, say in a corridor, they must each time exchange greetings and acknowledge the other person. Usually this is done with a bow and a smile, or a shortened form of the general greeting, **doomo**. **Doomo** is a multi-purpose word which means that one person sincerely acknowledges the other.

Regardless of how informal the context is, affection is seldom expressed by physical contact during greeting. Even handshaking is rarely used, although it is becoming more widespread, particularly among people who have spent time overseas. In general, however, a person is expected to bow, with the person of lower status bowing more deeply than the person of higher status.

> How do people greet each other in Australia?
>
> What part does body language play in greetings?
>
> Do greetings vary according to the relative age or status of the people involved? How does the degree of familiarity affect the greeting?
>
> Do greetings between the same two people vary according to the situation? If so, how?

Classroom Task

Over the next few days, keep a record of how Australians greet each other. Make a copy of the form on next page and fill it in according to your observations. Then explain what would happen in a similar situation in Japan. An example has been completed for you. Compare what you record with what other people in the class have recorded.

If you were giving advice to a group of newly arrived Japanese students about how to greet Australians, what would you tell them?

Participants	Place	Comments in Australia	Probable comments in Japan
Two colleagues	In front of lift	'Had a good weekend?' 'Yeah, quite good.' No special body language	Probably comment that other looks busy

Introductions

When introducing people, the relative status of the people involved is crucial in determining who is introduced first. In most situations, the younger person or the subordinate is first introduced, usually by a third party who provides such information as the person's name, company, and the relationship between the introducer and the person being introduced. The older person or superior then takes over the conversation by introducing him or herself. Name cards or ***meishi*** 名刺 are often exchanged in formal and semi-formal situations.

三友商事（株）	MITSUTOMO CO. LTD.
総務部　経理課	Business Administration Dept. • Accounting section
課長　山田　邦夫	Manager KUNIO YAMADA
東京都港区赤坂 5-2-3 電話　03　3（985）2222（内線 254）	5-2-3 Akasaka Minato–ward Tokyo Telephone: 03 3(985)2222 (Ext. 254)

Although exchange of name cards does not usually take place in informal settings, the basic rules described above still apply, with the younger person or subordinate being introduced first.

During introductions, a person's family name is used. The use of first names in formal and semi-formal situations is regarded as personal and therefore inappropriate.

Classroom task

In groups, act out each of the following situations, first in English, then as they would be done in Japan:

i) A friend visits you and you introduce him or her to your flatmate. You are all about the same age.

ii) At a party you introduce your friend to your boss.

iii) You want to introduce your mother to your friend.

What differences are there between Japanese and Australian introductions?

- Who is introduced first and why?
- What do you say when introducing someone? Name? Job?
- Who initiates the conversation after being introduced?
- Does the way people in the two cultures introduce each other tell you anything about what those cultures think is important.

Leave-taking

Australians who are invited to visit Japanese families are often astonished by what they see as everlasting leave-taking before the guest actually leaves. Mary Jones, who recently joined a Japanese firm, tells of her experience at a lunch party for the section in which she worked:

> We were ready to leave the house but everyone stood at the doorway and kept talking. The guests repeatedly expressed their gratitude for the invitation, for

the food and for the wonderful time they had had, while the host modestly denied that they had done anything. I must admit I was a little irritated towards the end. The hosts then came out to the gate to see us off and continued waving until we reached the corner. It was a real ritual!

Japanese leave-taking may indeed appear to be rather ceremonial. Nonetheless, it is an important aspect of social interaction which minimises the possibility of conflict right to the end. Japanese often find themselves at a loss when trying to take leave in the Australian context. They cannot find an expression in English that effectively allows them to avoid conflict. Some Japanese solve this problem by repeatedly saying 'thank you' to express their sincere appreciation.

Awkward moments may also occur in telephone calls. After the reasons for the call have been dealt with, most Japanese find it too abrupt and impersonal to simply hang up immediately. It is therefore usual to add a few words of enquiry about the family, or to apologise for taking up a person's time. Below is the closing stage of a telephone conversation between a teacher and a high school student, a call during which the student had reported about her new job:

(After the main points have been discussed)

S: *Hontoo ni o-isogashii tokoro ni o-denwa o sashiagete sumimasendeshita.*
'I am sorry to call you when you are busy.'

T: *Iie, doo itashimashite*
'That's no problem.'
Kazoku no minasan wa o genki desu ka
'Is your family well?'

S: *Hai, okagesamade*
'Yes, thank you, they are.'

T: *Kondo, mata asobi ni kite kudasai ne*
'Come and visit me sometime.'

S: *Arigatoo gozaimasu, zehi soo itashimasu*
'Thank you, I shall do so by all means.'

T: *Jaa, shigoto no hoo mo ganbatte ne*
'Well then, good luck with your work.'

S: *Hontoo ni iroiro to ki o tsukatte itadaite arigatoo gozaimasu*
'Thank you for being so caring.'

T: *Sorejaa, mata ne*
'Well then, see you sometime.'

S: *Hai, dewa shitsurei shimasu*
'Yes, excuse me.'

T: *Hai, doomo*
'OK, goodbye.'

Japanese students may feel impolite when they are using the less elaborate English leave-taking rituals.

> Many Japanese students feel clumsy and awkward during the opening and closing stages of interaction, and particularly when finishing a conversation. This is true even for advanced students whose English proficiency easily allows them to participate in conversations on issues such as politics and economics.
>
> Why do you think there is such a discrepancy between language proficiency in the sense of being able to exchange information and proficiency in the sense of social appropriateness?
>
> How would you design a syllabus to tackle such issues?

Classroom Tasks

■ Task 1 ■

Fumiko, a Japanese housewife in Australia, commented to an Australian friend that she often felt awkward when she was trying to finish a telephone conversation with an Australian. She didn't want to sound too abrupt, and she didn't want to sound clumsy or halting either.

Have you had similar experiences? Share your experiences with other members of the class.

How might you solve this problem?

■ Task 2 ■

Ask your teacher to record the ending of one of her telephone conversations with a friend. Alternatively, you could ask your flatmate, if you're sharing with an Australian, or one of your friends.

How do Australians finish off a telephone conversation?

> Task 2 *continued*
>
> Note down the phrases they use.
>
> How does it compare with how you would finish a conversation in Japan?
>
> Explain these differences to your teacher.
>
> ### ■ Task 3 ■
>
> In pairs, act out leave-taking in the following situations. First act the situation as it would occur in Australia and then as it would occur in Japan.
>
> What are the differences?
>
> i) Students leaving class.
>
> ii) People leaving work at the end of the day.
>
> iii) Two friends parting after a day out together.
>
> iv) Leaving a friend's home after a dinner party.

Agreeing, Disagreeing and Expressing Opinions

Problem solving in the West usually involves an exchange of opposing views. This is considered to be the fairest way of arriving at a solution. Such a process of problem solving seems rather aggressive to a Japanese.

The experiences of Mr Hosono, a newly arrived businessman, aptly illustrate the differences between Australia and Japan regarding the expression of opinions. One day a meeting was held to discuss the marketing of a new product. Ten people, all from different departments, were present. One of the section heads presented an outline of the marketing proposal. As soon as he had finished his presentation, he was, in Mr Hosono's words, attacked. A less senior member of another department raised some objections to certain aspects of the proposal. Her argument was then amplified by another speaker who raised further problems. Another point of view was put by a third speaker. Mr Hosono felt as if he were in the middle of a battlefield. What was even more puzzling was the establishment of 'peace' towards the end of the meeting. Having reached agreement, the participants smiled, exchanged a few jokes and generally acted as if the dispute had never taken place. Mr Hosono meanwhile felt that he had just been through an extremely aggressive confrontation.

> What aspects of this discussion do you think surprised Mr Hosono? What were his expectations?

Naturally, Japanese do express their opinions. They do agree and disagree with each other. But there are differences, sometimes subtle, sometimes quite great, in the way they go about doing it. First of all, one person does not openly and directly contradict another person's opinion. It is usual to start by making some favourable comments about the proposal or opinion under discussion. The disagreement itself then usually takes the form of a suggestion. It is considered more effective to allow a person time to reflect on their original statement rather than to directly object to it. Had Mr Hosono wished to present his own opinion in the meeting above, he would have probably phrased it something like this:

Soo desu ne. Kihon teki ni wa risoo teki na an da to omoimasu. Keredomo, genzai no ryuutsuumoo no koto o kangaemasuto, doyoobi no un-ei ga sukoshi kininarimasu ga ...'.

'Let's see ... basically, your proposal is ideal, but thinking about the existing marketing network, I'm a little concerned about operations on Saturdays ...'.

When Australians are faced with this kind of disagreement, they may be unsure of the point being made. They may also underestimate how strongly the disagreement is felt, treating it as minor when in fact a very serious objection is being raised. Gauging opinion from a suggestive comment may appear unnecessarily circuitous to those who are used to a more adversarial style of argument.

Conflict is the last thing Japanese expect in a discussion. It is for this reason that the ***ringi*** system — a bottom-up approach to decision-making — was created. This will be discussed in greater detail in Chapter 7: *The Concept of Harmony.*

> How do you think that Japanese attitudes to discussion outlined above might affect your Japanese students' participation in classroom discussion?
>
> If some Japanese women students, for example, are reluctant to take part in discussions, should the language teacher attempt to change this?
>
> How might you teach Australian attitudes to discussion?

INTERACTING IN SOCIETY 91

> **Classroom Tasks**
>
> ■ **Task 1** ■
>
> Watch one of the current affairs programs on Australian television, a program such as *Sixty Minutes or The Seven Thirty Report*. Select one of the discussions and note:
>
> i) How do people agree and disagree with each other? Are they direct or indirect in presenting their opinions?
>
> ii) What words or phrases do they use?
>
> iii) Does their intonation change when they are arguing? If so, how does it change?
>
> iv) How would you feel if you were taking part in an argument like this? What would you do?
>
> ■ **Task 2** ■
>
> Mr Fraser was visiting Japan to finalise a contract with a Japanese firm. On the day of his arrival he was taken to a restaurant and during dinner talked at length about the contract on what he thought was a social basis. He was therefore surprised when, in the meeting next day, the Japanese side began by saying, 'As we discussed last night ...'.
>
> What different assumptions did the two sides have about the status of the discussions in the restaurant and why?

Complimenting

When receiving a compliment, a person is expected to reply in a modest manner. This is not to say that the compliment is being rejected. Rather, a humble response has the effect of neutralising the potential embarrassment of being singled out. The person giving the compliment therefore expects to follow their initial compliment with reinforcement. Let's consider the conversation below. Takako has just passed her university entrance exams and is being complimented by her neighbour, Mrs Sato:

    Mrs Sato: *Gookaku omedetoo*
                        'Congratulations on your success in the exams.'

Takako:	*Yaa, un ga yokatta n desu yo*
	'Well, I was just lucky.'
Mrs Sato:	*Sonna koto nai wa yo. Isshookenmei benkyoo shita n da kara.*
	'No, no, it was because you studied so hard.'
Takako:	*Ee maa korekara shibaraku benkyoo o shinakute mo ii to omou to chotto hotto shimasu*
	'Yes, well, I feel a little relieved that I don't have to study for a while.'

The person who is giving the compliment tries to reinforce it after it has initially been declined. Japanese in Australia may feel, when some compliments such as those on clothes or on general physical appearance are accepted immediately, that the conversation is somehow unfinished. Australians learning Japanese may also have some awkward moments. After spending several months in Japan, one Australian student reported 'I just didn't know how to get rid of the tension after I'd paid this friend a compliment. I knew that I had to say something in reply to the their modesty, but I didn't know what, so I smiled.'

Compliments are more often exchanged among women, who tend to be better at expressing their admiration of others than men. Japanese men are usually very reserved in paying compliments, to the extent that one Australian married to a Japanese complained 'My husband wouldn't say anything whatever I cooked or whatever I wore!'

Classroom Tasks:

■ Task 1 ■

Toshiko was a Japanese student living in Sydney. She shared a flat with an Australian girl who always wore jeans and T-shirts. They suited her, but she often looked very boyish. One day, however, she was wearing a dress and she really looked great. Toshiko said, 'You look fantastic in that dress. Why don't you dress like that all the time?' Toshiko meant well, but her flatmate was obviously not very pleased.

Why was Toshiko's flatmate offended?

■ Task 2 ■

During their two-week holiday in Australia, Mr and Mrs Saito visited their Australian friend, Anne Parker. They complimented her on her flat, saying 'It's a beautiful flat. It's too good for you, Anne.' (*Anne, ni wa mottai nai kurai da ne.*) Anne was obviously hurt by this comment.

- Why was Anne upset by the comment?
- What would you advise Mr and Mrs Saito to do to make Anne feel better?
- How could Mr and Mrs Saito appropriately compliment Anne about her flat?

Asking for Permission

Having Junko as an exchange student, Mrs Heath was both impressed by the Japanese student's manners and irritated by her apparent inability to do anything without asking. 'May I take some orange juice from the fridge?'; 'May I use the washing machine?'; 'May I open the closet?'; 'May I go to the post office?' She appreciated Junko's efforts to be polite but wondered why she was so excessive about it.

Japanese are very conscious of the difference between their territory and that of others. They try to avoid infringing what they feel to be other people's territory. Junko felt that the fridge, the washing machine and the closet were all in the Heath's territory. Similarly, a decision on whether or not she could go to the post office lay in Mrs Heath's hands as she was the host mother. Junko was afraid of intruding if she did not first ask permission. Many Japanese are in fact shocked when Australians touch their possessions without permission. A Japanese student, for example, could not believe his eyes when an Australian friend joined him in the canteen and picked up his dictionary without first asking.

The necessity to ask permission in private does not extend to the public domain. Public places are not perceived to belong to anybody, so it is only recently that, for example, Japanese have begun asking 'Do you mind if I smoke?'

Power relationships also have a strong bearing on the appropriateness of asking for permission. Kenji, who works in a bank, comments that he would feel guilty if he left the office before his seniors. If he had planned to go out in the evening but his superior decided to work late, he would cancel his plans rather than seek permission to leave work early. It is taken for granted that work takes priority over private matters.

> If a concern not to infringe on others' territory underlies seeking permission in Japanese, what determines when Australians have to seek permission?

Classroom Tasks

■ Task 1 ■

How do you ask for permission in English?

In pairs, act out each of the following situations. Ask your teacher and other students to comment on the appropriateness of what you say and do.

How does an Australian's approach compare with what a Japanese might do in each situation?

a) You are going to attend your sister's wedding next month. Ask your boss for the day off.

b) You couldn't finish your assignment in time. Ask your teacher for an extension.

c) You are a student who works in a cake shop on Wednesdays and Thursdays. Next Thursday you have an important test, so you want to ask your colleague to swop shifts with you for that week. Your colleague works on Saturdays.

d) You are sitting with others in a waiting room waiting for a long distance train. It is very hot and you want to open the window.

e) You are visiting some friends and you feel like a cigarette.

> ■ **Task 2** ■
>
> Bob studies in a Japanese university. One day he went to make an appointment with his lecturer to discuss his assignment. The lecturer suggested three o'clock on Wednesday, saying he would be back from his lecture by then. Bob apologetically said that he had a dentist's appointment at that time and asked if a time on Thursday afternoon was possible. It was obvious that his lecturer was not pleased.
>
> Why was the lecturer not pleased?
>
> What should Bob have done?
>
> What would happen in the same situation in an Australian university?

Offering, Declining and Accepting

A Japanese couple was invited to dinner by an Australian family that lived next door. The couple were delighted by the invitation and accepted gladly. However, they went on to say, 'But won't it be too much trouble for you? You must be awfully busy ...'. The Australian couple interpreted this as a sign of reluctance to come to dinner.

The message the couple meant to convey was one of grateful acceptance together with some consideration for the Australian family. They wanted to say that they were very grateful for the invitation, especially because the Australian family was making an effort and going to trouble on their behalf.

What would have happened if the couple wanted to decline the invitation? Refusal usually involves giving reasons for the refusal. The actual word 'No' is seldom spoken in such an interaction. Participants therefore have to read each others' cues carefully. In translation, a refusal would sound something like this:

Ohta: *Raishuu no doyoobi no yoru ni o-shokuji ni irasshaimasen ka.*
Would you like to come to dinner on Saturday evening?

Itoh: *Arigatoo gozaimasu. Demo, sono hi wa inaka kara ryooshin ga dete kuru node.*
Thankyou, but my parents are coming to visit us on that day.

Ohta: *Jaa chotto muri desu ne. sorejaa zannen desu kedo, mata kondo ni shimashoo.*
It doesn't seem possible then. Well, it's a shame ... but let's make it some other time.

Itoh: *Sumimasen, sekkaku o-maneki itadaita noni ...*
Sorry, ... in spite of your sincere invitation ...

The act of offering is also subject to misunderstanding. When a person offers something, say a gift, they often make a negative comment about it. A phrase such as 'This is just a trivial gift and I don't know if you'll like it, but ...' is commonly heard during such an interaction. A woman might apologise for her cooking, saying 'This might not suit your taste', when she is serving dinner to her guests. However, it is important not to over-generalise. Speech varies according to the situation and the participants in the interaction. Among friends, it would be common to say something more direct, such as 'I found this book at the local bookshop and I thought you'd be interested'.

> **How do Australians decline offers? Is refusal generally indicated directly or indirectly? How does the refusal vary with the relationship of the participants in the interaction?**

Classroom Tasks

■ Task 1 ■

Susan rang her Japanese friend Takeshi to invite him to a picnic the following weekend. As Takeshi didn't have a car, Susan offered to collect him.

Susan:	So, I'll come round at eleven o'clock, OK?
Takeshi:	OK. I'll be waiting at the corner.
Susan:	Why? I can come to your place. It's no problem.
Takeshi:	Oh, then I'll be standing at the gate.
Susan:	Look, it's cold out. Why don't you wait inside? It's really no problem ... unless you don't want me to come to your flat ...

What is happening in this situation? What message did Takeshi intend to convey?

As a language teacher, how could you help Takeshi avoid such misunderstandings?

> ■ **Task 2** ■
>
> What would you do in the following situations?
>
> Compare the Japanese and the Australian responses. Are there any differences?
>
> Choose one of the situations and act it out.
>
> a) You are visiting your friend's house to return a book. Unfortunately, your friend is out, but his mother invites you in for a cup of tea.
>
> b) You are giving your next door neighbour a cake that you've just baked. It smells very good.
>
> c) Your boss has invited the whole section to a sushi bar. Unfortunately, you don't like raw fish. The waiter is taking orders.
>
> d) You are standing at a bus stop when your teacher drives by and sees you. He stops his car and says he can give you a lift. He is going in your direction.

Apologising

'I wonder how many times the average Japanese would say ***sumimasen*** (I'm sorry), in their lives. You can get around just fine as long as you know that word.' So an Australian working for a Japanese company summarised his experience. He went on to say that the Japanese staff apologised if they were using the photocopier when someone else walked into the photocopy room, they apologised for asking where something was, for using the computer if someone else came along, when being served a cup of tea ... the list seemed never ending.

A sense of guilt accompanies the gratitude felt by Japanese when something is done for them. Thinking of the trouble that the other person might have gone to, many Japanese feel they should do something to compensate. This guilt extends to any situation where one person feels he may have caused another trouble. If, for example, you offer a lift to a Japanese friend, they will feel not only appreciative of the kindness, but also guilty because of the inconvenience caused.

Sumimasen has a second meaning. It also means 'Thank you'. ***Sumimasen*** is the negative form of ***sumimasu*** and literally means 'not completed'. The speaker feels that something has to be done in order to complete the interaction between himself and the other person or people in the situation. For example, if Mrs

Hayashi's neighbour took her washing in for her because it started to rain while she was out, Mrs Hayashi would say **sumimasen**, meaning 'I'm sorry I caused you so much trouble'. She would feel grateful and guilty at the same time.

If, however, the feeling of gratitude or guilt is extremely strong, then the strongest gesture of apology is to remain silent. By not uttering a word, a person implicitly allows the other party to decide on the appropriate action or reaction. Most importantly, they do not seek to offer excuses or reasons. To do so appears to be attempting to avoid responsibility.

Classroom Task

Masao Sakamoto teaches English in a public school in Japan. One day, a Japanese student and an exchange student from Australia broke a classroom window while playing sport. Masao called the students to the staff room. Before Masao asked any questions, Mark, the Australian student, explained what had happened:

Masao:	Sit down.
Mark:	I'm sorry, sir. We were practising basketball and ...
Toshio:	(looking down) Ummm ...
Mark:	I missed the net and the ball went through the window. I'm sorry, Mr Sakamoto. It was an accident ... It'll never happen again. We'll be more careful next time ...
Toshio:	(looking down) Ummmm ...

What do you think Mr Sakamoto might have thought about Mark?

Why didn't Toshio say anything? And why did Mark say so much?

If this had happened in an Australian school, what would an Australian teacher have thought about Toshio's silence and Mark's explanations?

How would you explain Mark's behaviour to Mr Sakamoto?

How would you explain Toshio's silence to an Australian teacher?

Thanking

As we saw in the previous section, **sumimasen** can often be used to thank. There is, however, another common word that translates as 'thank you'. **Arigatoo** only translates as 'thank you'. While **sumimasen** is used in formal and semi-formal situations, **arigatoo** is more frequently employed in informal settings. Hierarchy and the degree of intimacy prevailing determine which is 'formal' and which 'informal'.

When a younger person or a subordinate thanks an older person or a superior, the humble form **sumimasen** is appropriate, while in the reverse situation **arigatoo** may more frequently be heard. This applies to settings such as the school, the office or in public places. Within the family, however, it does not apply. **Sumimasen** sounds too distant even when considering the major status differences between parents and children.

Another feature of thanking in Japanese is that people express their gratitude even after the lapse of an extended period of time. In fact it constitutes an important part of a conversation. For example, while talking to an Australian couple, a Japanese couple thanked them for a dinner party that had occurred two months before. The Australians did not at first understand what they were being thanked for. Having already been thanked on the evening itself, these further words seemed uncalled for and excessive. For the Japanese couple, on the other hand, acknowledgement of favours received formed a significant component of the conversation, particularly in greeting.

Classroom Task

Make a copy of the chart overleaf and use it over the next week to record when people say 'thankyou' and when they say 'I'm sorry'.

In the right hand columns, record when you hear Japanese use **sumimasen** and **arigatoo**. In the left hand ones, record when Australians use 'I'm sorry' and 'thankyou'.

At the end of the week, compare your charts with other people in your class. What similarities and what differences do you notice between the way Australians thank and apologise and the way Japanese do?

	AUSTRALIA		JAPAN	
	Situation	Phrase	Situation	Phrase
Thanks	Milkbar: getting change	Asst: Thanks Cust: Thanks		
Apology				

Complaining

Because of the golden rule of Japanese interaction, 'avoid conflict', complaining is difficult for most Japanese. In order to avoid an emotional clash, Japanese tend to imply a message rather than openly complain.

Suppose you are a student studying for an examination. You are trying to concentrate but are annoyed by the sound of the piano being played by the girl next door. Your complaint to her would be phrased something like this:

Student: *ano ... sumimasen piano no koto na n desuga*
Well, it's about the piano ...

Neighbour: *piano? ano ... uchi no piano desu ka.*
Piano? You mean our piano?

Student: *ee ...*
Yes.

Neighbour: *otaku made kikoemasu ka.*
Does the noise travel to your place?

Student: *ee ... itsumo nara kamawanai n desu kedo, ima choodo shiken no tame no benkyoo o shite iru node ...*
Yes, ... it doesn't worry me normally but it's just because I'm studying for exams at the moment, so ...

Neighbour: *aa soo deshita ka*
Oh, I see.

Student: *ima made amari benkyoo shite inakatta node, chotto ganbaranakereba to omotte*
I haven't been studying much until now, so I thought I should really try hard now.

Neighbour: *wakarimashita. musume ni itte, chiisai oto de hikaseru yoo ni shimashoo*
Alright, I will tell my daughter to play more quietly.

Student: *sumimasen ga yoroshiku onegai shimasu*
I'm sorry about this, but if you wouldn't mind ...

Even if dissatisfaction exists, complaints are not made at all in some cases. It is often considered more virtuous to endure hardship than to create an uncomfortable situation. A Japanese student once amazed his flatmates by suddenly announcing that he was moving out. He said that he couldn't bear the untidiness of his flatmates, but hadn't said a single word about it until the day he declared that he was moving. As he said, 'I didn't want to make a fuss and make everyone feel awkward.'

The above examples were all set against a background of casual interaction.

However, outside this framework, Japanese complain openly and directly. In a shop, for example, complaints about service or quality are openly voiced. That is, when there is no on-going relationship between the participants in an interaction then making complaints is acceptable.

> When do people complain in Australia?
>
> If the Japanese attitude toward complaining is linked to the desire to maintain harmony, what values in Australian culture might be linked to the Australian attitude to complaining?

Classroom Task

Natsuko shares a flat with two Australian girls. The two are usually good company, but they have a few habits that Natsuko finds very hard to take. One of them always avoids cleaning the flat and the other never washes up after cooking. Natsuko normally ends up doing the extra work as she can't stand leaving the place so untidy. She hasn't said anything to her flatmates as she doesn't want to upset them. She is thinking of finding a new place to live but feels a little reluctant about leaving her otherwise-pleasant flatmates.

What advice would you give Natsuko?

Natsuko in fact left the flat one month later.

Was there anything the two Australians should have done in order to prevent her leaving?

What advice would you give the two Australians in order to prevent something similar happening again?

Requesting Assistance

In requesting assistance, Japanese usually provide the reasons assistance is needed without necessarily making a direct request. If, for example, a student were asking his teacher to provide him with a reference for a job, he would say something like, 'I'm applying for a new job. I think I need a reference.'

When someone is seeking assistance in a formal situation, such as at school or in a company, it is considered appropriate to approach the immediate superior even if the actual decision about whether or not to give the assistance will ultimately be made at a higher level. The request has to be handed up the hierarchy and violation of this step-by-step approach may be resented by those in intermediate positions. One Japanese manager, for example, expressed his anger when one of his staff members contacted the personnel manager regarding her salary without referring the matter to him first. He commented, 'Of course I am not in charge of salaries, but I should be informed of everything that is going on because I'm in charge of the section. I think this is only basic politeness.'

Classroom Task

Masao has just started a job with an Australian company. He wants to improve his computing skills and the company offers a range of training programs, one of which Masao feels would be very useful for him.

How do you think Masao should go about applying for the course?

Who should he speak to and what should he do?

If the company had been a Japanese company, would Masao follow the same procedure?

What, if any, differences are there?

Asking for Information

In comparing ways of asking for information in Australia and Japan, the difference lies not so much in how, but when, to ask for information. Let me give you a concrete example.

An American university lecturer gave a speech at a seminar in Tokyo. During the question-and-answer session that followed, very few questions were raised. The lecturer was disappointed by this reaction, thinking that the audience had judged his paper to be of little interest. Later, however, when the seminar was over he was, as he put it, deluged by people wanting to talk to him. The exchange of question and answer took place on an individual basis.

Although in many Western cultures asking questions is encouraged as a sign of active interaction, this is not the case in Japan. People feel inhibited from asking questions, especially in formal situations such as seminars, for fear that their questions may seem inappropriate or are of no concern to others. Needless to say, however, communication styles vary from person to person. The younger generation, for example, is more accustomed to interactive settings and are less hesitant to speak out in public.

In everyday situations such as service encounters, however, people do not hesitate to ask. As in Australia, polite forms which are the equivalent of 'Could you tell me ...' and 'please' are used.

Classroom Activity

What would you do in the circumstances described below. Discuss your answers with a partner and then compare them with the answers of other people in the class.

What would an Australian do in the same situation?

i)   You didn't understand the teacher's explanation during class.

ii) You want to ask the price of a product in an expensive shop.

iii) Your employer has just explained how to operate the new office fax, but you still don't understand.

iv) You are on a tour of Sydney and you want to ask the tour guide several questions.

Expressing Ability

When asked how well she could play the piano, a Japanese student answered, 'A little.' When she was asked to play, she began playing a piece by Chopin.

Japanese tend to understate their abilities when asked because a high value is placed on modesty. At the same time, a person may also be attempting to pre-empt a negative judgment.

The inquirer would not normally accept the speaker's negative evaluation, but would tend to challenge the assessment:

    Takako: Yuko, you play tennis very well, don't you?
    Yuko: Yes, a little
    Takako: I don't believe that. I heard that you were very good.

> How do Australians express their ability?
>
> Are they expected to overstate, understate or to give a relatively objective assessment?
>
> What problems would you expect Japanese speakers to have both in interpreting the Australian way of talking about abilities and in themselves talking about their own abilities?
>
> How might your understanding of Japanese expectations influence your teaching in this respect?

Classroom Task

How would you respond to the following questions:

i) At a job interview for a secretarial position, you are asked about your typing speed. You actually type about 50 words/minute.

ii) An Australian person asks you how much you know about Australian history. Actually you know quite a lot because you read a number of books before you came.

iii) You are asked what sports you play and how well.

iv) A Japanese acquaintance asks you how good your English is.

Now ask an Australian the same questions. (Remember to first change the words 'Australian' and 'Japanese' where necessary!)

What differences do you find in the answers?

Explain the reasons for the Japanese answers to your teacher and ask her to explain the Australian answers to you.

Expressing Emotions

Expression of emotion in public is generally not encouraged in Japan. An attempt is made to conceal one's emotions from others, especially negative emotions such as anger or boredom.

Suppressed emotions, even when a person is furious, may be concealed behind a smile. Such discreet expression of emotion is considered virtuous. Many

Japanese remark that, when in serious discussions or conversations, Australians don't smile. Some find this serious demeanour disconcerting and perhaps indicative of hostility.

This attitude is also reflected in the language. In English, it is possible to attribute emotions to anyone: that is, one can say, 'I am sad' and/or 'He is sad'. In Japanese, firm statements about the emotional state of a third person cannot be made. Rather, one is obliged to say, 'It seems he is sad'.

Having said this, however, it is important to note that while most Japanese are reluctant to openly express emotions, it varies from individual to individual. Younger people in particular are more likely to reveal their emotional state than older people.

Classroom Task

Mrs Stewart works for a municipal council in Sydney. Last month, she received a delegation from a Japanese city which was about to sign a sister-city agreement with the municipality. Mrs Stewart found all the delegates pleasant and easy to get on with on a social basis. However, business was another matter. Whenever they were discussing an important issue with her, the delegates, all men, kept on smiling for no apparent reason. As there was nothing funny about the discussions, Mrs Stewart decided, on the basis of what she had read about Japan, that the men were patronising her. She felt that they were laughing at her because she was a woman. Mrs Stewart quickly began dreading her meetings with the delegation.

Was Mrs Stewart right in her interpretation of the delegates' behaviour?

How would you explain their behaviour to Mrs Stewart?

Have you yourself ever experienced anything similar in your interactions with people from another culture?

Aizuchi or 'Back-channelling'

In conversation, Japanese speakers tend to interject comments while the speaker is still speaking. When listening to a Japanese on the telephone, it is common to hear constant signals such as **hai**, 'yes', or **ee**, 'yeah' which indicate that the listener is still listening.

Such short interjections are called ***aizuchi***, which may be translated as back-channelling. ***Aizuchi*** is thrown into the conversation after almost every phrase: according to researchers, about twenty times a minute. When a Japanese speaker carries this habit over into English, some Australians may interpret it as repeated attempts to interrupt, and conclude that the listener is impolite.

The functions of ***aizuchi*** are mainly to acknowledge that the listener is interested in what the speaker has to say and to encourage the speaker to keep on speaking. Its absence may cause the speaker anxiety as they may feel the listener is not interested. Here is a conversation between two friends about their experiences in Australia. Note that the square brackets indicate overlapping speech or mannerisms.

Taro:	Well ...
Jun:	Yeah ...
Taro:	There are times ...
Jun:	nh ...
Taro:	that I feel awkward living [nodding] in Australia.
Jun:	Yeah.
Taro:	You know [yeah, nh] it's a foreign land.
Jun:	That's right.
Taro:	Language ...
Jun:	Yeah ...
Taro:	that's one thing.
Jun:	Yes, I'm sure. In Japan, [nodding] I was quite confident about my English.
Taro:	Yeah, your English is good.
Jun:	but having arrived here ...
Taro:	nh ...
Jun:	there are times when I can't make myself understood.
Taro:	Is that right?
Jun:	Especially [nodding] in places like [nodding] shops [yeah] ... and [nodding] in the bus [yeah] ...

By constantly acknowledging each other's contribution, the two co-operate in building a conversation. When speaking English, however, pauses allowing for ***aizuchi*** may not occur and the Japanese listener may opt for constant silent nodding.

> How do you signal your interest and attention in English?
>
> Do you think such features of conversation should be taught in class or is it more likely they will be unconsciously picked up?
>
> If you taught them, how would you do so?

Classroom Task

When people are talking to each other, how does the listener show that he or she is paying attention?

Record a few minutes of a conversation between you and a Japanese friend. Listen to the recording together — how does the listener indicate that they are paying attention?

Do Australians do the same thing? Watch a couple of Australians as they are talking. How do they indicate that they are listening?

How would you explain the Japanese method to an Australian?

Do You Mean 'Yes' or 'No'?

Where a negative sentence is concerned, the use of 'yes' and 'no' in Japanese is opposite to that of English. If you ask your student 'Don't you understand?' and your student answers 'Yes', you should not feel relieved, believing that there is no problem. 'Yes' as the answer to a negative question in Japanese means, 'Yes, your statement is correct. I do not understand.' The basic rule is that the listener will answer 'yes' or 'no' according to whether they judge the speaker's statement to be correct or not:

> Don't you like eggs?
> Yes = Your statement is correct. I don't like eggs.
> No = Your statement is incorrect. I do like eggs.

The issue of 'yes' and 'no' may be further complicated by the fact that Japanese tend to avoid direct answers. Ambiguous statements are preferred and people depend on the listener's intuition to judge the real intention of an utterance. Thus, a phrase like 'I will consider it positively', once used by a Japanese politician to the

President of the United States can cause great misunderstanding on both sides. What the Japanese politician meant was that he would make an effort, but at this stage the answer was 'No'. The President understood that while the answer was not yet absolutely definite, the proposal would be favourably considered, with a high probability of a final 'Yes.'

'Yes' also serves as an acknowledgement to the speaker by the listener — 'Yes, I am listening to you.' Look at the following dialogue between two colleagues:

Takahashi: About yesterday's meeting ...
Yoshida: **Hai** 'Yes'
Takahashi: I really think we need to go over the figures again.
Yoshida: **Hai** 'Yes'

Here, Yoshida is not agreeing with Takahashi, rather he is just indicating that he is taking notice of what is being said. This use of 'yes', when transferred into English, also has considerable potential for creating misunderstanding!

Some General Considerations on Japanese Interaction Patterns

We have now examined many features of Japanese interactive patterns. As you might have noted, direct realisations of functions are often avoided. If, for example, you wanted someone to do something, you would tend to avoid direct expressions such as 'Could you' or 'I'd like/I want you to ...'. Instead, remarks explaining why you needed that person to do something would be made and the listener would be left to deduce the actual intention.

This type of interaction pattern warns us that what is stated in words may be different from what a person actually means. In the case of Japanese, intentions are usually not directly displayed, the main reason being the very strong desire to avoid conflict.

CHAPTER ■ SEVEN

VALUES THINKING IN SOCIETY

In this chapter we will study the value systems which influence peoples' ways of thinking.

We tend to take it for granted that the values inherent in our own culture are universal. Each of us has expectations about how others should behave and deviation from expected patterns of speech or behaviour can cause bewilderment and even resentment.

I myself experienced some confusion during the early stages of my teaching career in Australia. I was bewildered by the informal atmosphere of the classroom. The students approached me in such a familiar manner, quite at odds with teacher/student roles to which I had been accustomed in Japan. In the beginning, it seemed that the students' approach indicated a lack of respect. Obviously, this was not so: rather, their attitude was indicative of the co-operation between teacher and student that they believed was necessary for class activities to be carried out smoothly.

As many people are aware, the same utterances and actions can be interpreted differently according to the values by which they are judged. Different cultures stress different values and therefore interpret behaviours in different ways. In the following sections, we will look at several aspects of the Japanese value system which are prone to be misinterpreted by non-Japanese.

The Concept of the Individual

They think, therefore I am.' An English person made this sarcastic remark about the Japanese people after having lived in Japan for several years. Descartes, he claimed, could not have left us his famous proposition *Cogito ergo sum* had he be born in Japan. It is true that Japanese are extremely conscious of what others think of them. Spontaneous action may be inhibited for fear of criticism by others. Needless to say, such a tendency is present in any society; what is being considered here is the degree to which it is present.

From childhood, the Japanese are taught to notice how others respond to their speech and actions. When an adult scolds a child, for example, typical phrases used are 'You'll be laughed at if you do that' or 'Stop crying, look, your friend is looking at you.'

Socially, this intense consciousness of others' opinions is captured in words such as **sekentei**, 'social decency', and **teisai**, 'social appearance'. A frequently heard expression is **sekentei ga warui**, 'it appears socially indecent.' Such concern about social judgment tends to take precedence over individual expression.

The Role of the State

Until the end of the Second World War, the interests of the individual were suppressed under the patriarchal system. Under this system, the state was compared to one large family. The word **kokka**, the Japanese equivalent of 'state', consists of two **kanji**, meaning 'country' and 'house' respectively. The individual was encouraged to ignore selfish self-interest and serve the country. The Imperial Rescript on Education stated 'With loyalty and courage fulfil the wish of the Emperor.' Self-sacrifice was taught as a virtue. One of the subjects taught at school, **shuuyoo**, 'self discipline and national morality', enforced patriotism. It taught that the role of the individual was not to seek fulfilment as an independent being, but rather to be a virtuous sacrifice for the good of the country.

When the New Constitution was promulgated after the war, a reaction against pre-war nationalism occurred, especially in the field of education. Today, Japanese are not encouraged to be militantly patriotic and in fact many people, especially the young, are quite indifferent to the claims of state and nation.

The Concept of Harmony — Wa 和

Wa or 'harmony' amongst people is the basis of Japanese society. Japanese are extremely sensitive to any possible conflict, and its avoidance can be observed in various aspects of Japanese culture.

When Japanese students arrive in Australia for the first time, they often feel shocked by the small, animated discussions which take place in many situations, such as those between friends or workmates and between members of the family. When a problem or misunderstanding occurs between two Australians, the most common way of dealing with it is an attempt to 'talk it out'. Opinions are exchanged so that each knows exactly what the other is thinking. The purpose of such talks, of course, is to solve the problem. However, for Japanese, such problem-solving talks can appear more as battles. Self-assertiveness is often perceived as aggression.

In order to avoid conflict in formal situations, as in business offices, the **ringi** system arose. When a decision needs to be made, such as on a new sales strategy, a proposal is made in writing by someone from the lower levels of management. The proposal document is then circulated around the office, normally up through the hierarchy, in order to obtain approval at each level of management. The final decision is made at top managerial level, based on approval of the document at all other levels. As the document is circulated, its initiator approaches each level privately to explain the plan. Any necessary changes, or even a total rejection of the proposal, are negotiated at the preliminary stages when opinions can be, and are, directly stated and discussed. Such groundwork, in which the intentions and opinions of each level are privately confirmed, is called **nemawashi**, which literaly means 'digging, cutting and binding around the roots before transplanting the tree.'

Decision-making after such preliminary groundwork is very commonly observed in Japanese companies. Unlike Western negotiations, where opposing viewpoints are discussed in a general meeting, Japanese use the ***ringi*** and ***nemawashi*** systems to maintain harmony and avoid conflict.

Wa is also celebrated as a virtue in many sayings. ***Washite doozezu***, meaning 'Harmonise with others, yet do not compromise spiritually' is a characteristic expression of the Japanese attitude towards harmony. The saying originally comes from the Analects of Confucius, a work which has strongly influenced Japanese thinking.

The Importance of Reciprocity

As you look carefully into cultural customs and practices, you will discover a hidden meaning common to seemingly haphazard cultural practices. One such example is the exchange of gifts in Japanese society, the reciprocal nature of such giving maintaining balanced relationships.

Twice a year, in summer and towards the end of the year, people send gifts to those who have helped them, or those to whom they owe some obligation that needs to be repaid. A person's superior in the office, clients, teachers, the go-between who arranged their marriage, are all people normally on the list for gift-giving. You may object to the custom by saying that these people have already been paid, and it is true that they have been offered a monetary reward. However, the reciprocity discussed here is a psychological one. Many Japanese feel obliged to compensate for the benefits they have received.

You may have noticed Japanese honeymooners frantically buying incredible numbers of gifts, or newly married couples staggering out of shops weighed down by huge piles of shopping bags. The scene may appear rather strange to those who have no knowledge of the Japanese concept of reciprocity. Gifts bought on the honeymoon are mainly to be given to important guests who came to the wedding, to relatives and to those friends and acquaintances who have given the couple ***senbetsu*** or send-off gifts. In this way, the sense of psychological duty is alleviated and relationships kept balanced.

The concept of reciprocity is well expressed in the word ***giri***, which designates the sense of justice with regard to human relationships. If a person has received a kindness, it is their duty to repay this kindness, regardless of the inconvenience it may cause them. Neglect of ***giri*** is considered disgraceful. Suppose you were a student working in close contact with your lecturers, receiving their support and tuition. This relationship creates a sense of ***giri*** in which you, as the student, feel obliged to express your gratitude to your teachers. Consequently, you feel inhibited from acting in any way which may be contrary to your teachers' wishes. There is an expression, ***on o ada de kaesu***, or 'repaying kindness with evil', which reflects the way in which failure to observe ***giri*** is likely to be strongly criticised by society.

The Importance of Education

Until the end of the Second World War, the privileged class, consisting of the aristocracy and the plutocracy, exercised power over the whole nation. Politically, the aristocracy occupied the majority of seats in the Upper House of the Diet, and economically, the ***zaibatsu*** were the most powerful financial bodies. Beneath these two privileged groups were the commoners, many of whom were condemned to poverty because of the high rents charged for farming land. Social mobility was very limited.

After the Second World War, when the class system was abolished and the ***zaibatsu*** liquidated, fundamental human rights, including the right to receive an education, were promised under the new constitution. Through land reform, large landholdings were confiscated and redistributed among the peasants. Thus a so-called egalitarian society was established.

In today's Japan, more than 90 per cent of the population categorise themselves as middle-class. This high figure can be ascribed to the fact that, due to the education system, anyone can rise up the social scale by, for example, graduating from a top-ranking university.

The real possibility of such success encourages many Japanese to great efforts in their education. Society also praises people who, through perseverance, succeed in their lives. The extraordinary competition of the entrance examinations, often called ***juken jigoku*** or 'the entrance examination hell', is a reflection of these values.

The Importance of Age

Kame no koo yori toshi no koo, meaning 'the older, the wiser', depicts the Japanese attitude towards age. Some anthropologists explain this as a legacy of an agrarian society, in which traditions were handed down from older people to the next generation. Japanese certainly respect age. In public places such as public transport, it is not for women but for the elderly that people give up their seats.

Promotion is often awarded on the basis of age. Previously, it was rare for young people to attain high positions at the expense of older people. This was because, if such an event happened, an uncomfortable situation arose as two key social conventions, relating to modesty before superiors and older people, were brought into conflict. While the needs of large companies have in fact resulted in younger people being promoted, the problem of how to resolve this conflict remains.

The importance of age is also reflected in the use of language. Honorific expressions are used when young people or subordinates are talking to older people or superiors. An English teacher recounted her astonishment at the behaviour of two of her students. The two were placed in the same class and appeared to be almost the same age. On the first day, both of them were equally polite to each other. However, as soon as they found out that there was in fact one year's difference in their ages, the degree of formality between them changed. The younger one became very polite, while the older one adopted a big sister-like manner. The reason that Japanese ask a person's age on first acquaintance may also be ascribed to the fact that language and social attitude are determined by the relative ages of speaker and listener.

The Concepts of *Uchi* and *Soto*

Uchi and ***soto***, literally translated as 'inside' and 'outside', are important in describing the Japanese consciousness of territory.

Masako, a Japanese student sharing a flat with Elizabeth, recently decided to move out and to find a flat with another Japanese student. However, she and Elizabeth got on well together and kept in touch. One day, Elizabeth invited Masako to dinner and was surprised by her change in manner. She kept asking permission for everything. 'Can I use the bathroom?', 'Can I sit here?', 'Can I have a look at that book?'. Elizabeth thought, 'She used to live here. She knows I don't mind those things', and finally asked Masako why she was asking so much. Masako explained that she would feel as if she were intruding on Elizabeth's territory unless she sought permission.

This territory-consciousness is seen in the language, especially in the demonstrative pronouns **kore**, **sore** and **are** meaning respectively 'this', 'that' and 'that over there'. Unlike English demonstratives which indicate relative distance or act as noun substitutes, Japanese demonstratives not only indicate distance but also identify the territory to which an object belongs.

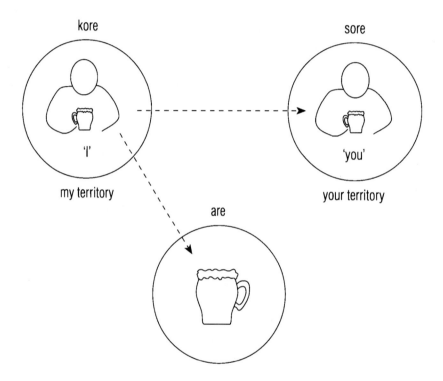

As the chart above demonstrates, **kore** refers to the speaker's own beer, or the beer which is in the speaker's territory. **Sore**, on the other hand, refers to the listener's beer or the beer which is in the listener's territory. **Are** indicates beer that does not belong either to the speaker ('I') or the listener ('you'). It may be another person's beer or it may simply be a beer which is sitting on a counter. Demonstrative pronouns in fact reflect very clearly the Japanese consciousness of a boundary separating their territory from that of others.

The use of honorific terms is also related to the concepts of **uchi** and **soto**. Let us take the example of an office situation. Miss Kinoshita is Mr Nomura's secretary. Within his section, she is expected to use the polite form, particularly when speaking to Mr Nomura, her superior. Here, she is 'inside' and Mr Nomura is 'outside'. However, when she goes to another section of the same company, she has to use the humble form to refer both to herself and to Mr Nomura, because they are now both 'inside' compared with the people of the other section, who are 'outside'. The same rule applies when Miss Kinoshita talks to people from another company.

The concepts of **uchi** and **soto** pervade every aspect of Japanese life. An individual defines him or herself as **uchi**, 'inside' a group and feels secure about being within rather than outside the boundary.

> If the recognition of hierarchic relations and the maintenance of harmony are key Japanese values, what do you think are the key Australian values?
>
> How are these values reflected in our day-to-day communication?

> Do you think the discussion and exploration of the values of a culture have a place in the language classroom?
>
> Do you see any dangers in such discussions?
>
> How would you cope with the dangers you identify?

Classroom Tasks

■ Task 1 ■

Many Australians feel that, today, the Union Jack, the British flag, should no longer feature on the Australian flag as most Australians now have no ties with Britain. They say Australia needs a new flag.

Design a new flag for Australia, one that you think truly represents Australia.

When you have finished, explain your design to the class. Why do you think your flag really represents what Australia is?

■ **Task 2** ■

It is often claimed that the two fundamental values of Australian culture are individualism and egalitarianism. Do you agree? Why or why not?

How do you think these values are reflected in daily life?

■ **Task 3** ■

Divide the class into several groups and ask each group to select a different Australian banknote.

In groups, discuss the following questions:
i) Who or what is illustrated on the banknote?
ii) Why do you think the Australian government chose these particular people and these particular incidents to illustrate bank notes?

Prepare a poster that explains what is illustrated on your group's note and why you think it was chosen.

When you have finished, compare your poster with those of other groups.

What do the people and events illustrated on Australia's banknotes tell you about Australian values?

Extension

The same thing can be done with Japanese banknotes and the values compared.

■ **Task 4** ■

It is often claimed that Japanese and Australian values are completely different, and in some ways this is true. However, we also share common values and common ways of behaving.

Over the next week, pay careful attention to what is going on around you. Watch people at work, on the train and in the shops. Watch them on television and in schools. How many values and ways of behaving can you find that Australians and Japanese share?

Report back to the class on what you find.

Which do you think are more important, the similarities or the differences?

■ Task 5 ■

Mr and Mrs Takeda were invited to dinner at the Edwards' house. When the Edwards' son, Ken, aged twelve, helped clear away the dishes, Mrs Takeda commented that he was a very helpful boy. She then asked him how he liked school. The conversation went like this:

Ken:	Oh, it's not bad ...
Mrs Takeda:	You must be very good at school.
Ken:	Mmmm ... not really ...
Mrs Edwards:	No, he really prefers playing sport.
Mrs Takeda:	Oh, what sport do you play?
Ken:	Soccer. We beat a really good team last week.
Mrs Takeda:	You must be good then.
Ken:	Oh, the team's really good, and we practise a lot. Twice a week. And we've got a good coach.
Mrs Edwards:	Yes, he really likes soccer. Typical kid, his school work's OK, but he's really good at sport.

How does Mrs Edwards really feel about her son's liking for sport? Is she praising him or criticising him?

If the same conversation took place about a Japanese boy in Japan, would you think the boy was being praised or criticised?

Are there any differences in the way the two cultures would interpret the same conversation?

CHAPTER ■ EIGHT

THE JAPANESE STUDENT IN THE CLASSROOM

English Education in Japan

English is a compulsory subject in both junior and senior high schools. Most Japanese therefore study English for at least six years, for an average of about three hours a week. However, even after spending enormous amounts of time studying English, very few students learn to speak it.

English education basically focuses not on English as a means of communication but on teaching about English. The conventional grammar/translation approach employed concentrates on developing skills such as the translation of English passages into Japanese, grammatical understanding and the composition of English sentences using that grammatical knowledge.

Given such training, Japanese students are, in general, well-versed in grammatical terminology. An Australian teacher who has taught in Japanese schools commented that Japanese students have a better grasp of English grammar than the average native speaker. In pronunciation, students are familiar with the International Phonetic Alphabet, which is used in textbooks from an early stage.

Though they have a passive knowledge of English, very few Japanese students can use it for active communication. Many language teachers in Japanese schools are aware that communicative teaching needs to be introduced into the English curriculum. They are hindered however by obstacles such as the importance of the university entrance examinations and class sizes. Entrance examinations in general focus on grammatical knowledge and the vocabulary of English, tested through such question types as cloze passages and translations. Naturally, teachers are expected to prepare students for these examinations.

Class sizes are also a matter of concern for language teachers. Under present circumstances, where an average class contains forty-five or more students, interaction between teacher and students is difficult. Consequently, English teaching, like the teaching of other subjects, tends to be done lecture-style.

Attitudes to Learning

In general, Japanese believe that learning requires discipline and perseverance, and does not coincide with fun. One student voiced the feelings of many when she complained:

> I came to Australia to study English, but teachers here don't teach us anything. We play games and do role plays. We are not even given a text book ...

Learning is a static activity for many Japanese. It involves sitting at a desk receiving knowledge, taking notes and memorising them. This is not to say, however, that Japanese are passive in their attitude to learning. On the contrary, Japanese are independent active learners with study skills cultivated throughout schooling. They are trained to prepare for the lesson, to listen to the teacher in the classroom and to review the lesson by memorising relevant material. In an English language classroom, for example, students normally look up new vocabulary and translate passages before attending the lesson. Afterwards, the lesson is reviewed by memorising new grammatical structures and vocabulary. Because of such study habits, Japanese students often feel insecure when they don't have materials prior to the lesson. Similarly, interactive lessons are often perceived as 'playing'.

In the Japanese classroom, listening is emphasised as one of the main methods of learning, while student contributions are discouraged. Students are generally expected to speak only when asked by the teacher. When asking questions, it is considered polite to wait until the teacher has completed his or her explanation, sometimes five or ten minutes before the bell rings. Being used to this system, many Japanese students at Australian universities express surprise when they see Australian students raising their hands before the lecturer has finished speaking. For them, such behaviour appears to be infringing on the lecturer's time. Consequently, Japanese students tend to ask questions privately after the end of class. While some Australian teachers have complained that this is unfair to other students who should also have the opportunity to hear the answer, Japanese students would not see the situation in this way. They would more probably feel that they are not wasting the lecturer's public time by asking their own private questions.

The Roles of Teacher and Student

Traditionally, a teacher is respected not only as someone who has a wide knowledge of an academic subject, but also as someone who is a model of morality. As teachers are looked up to, so also are they expected to look after their students in matters other than their own sphere of specialisation.

Students are divided into classes which are called 'home rooms. Each class has a home room teacher who takes charge of the students' welfare and discipline. Every year at the start of the new term, the home room teacher visits each student's home to learn about the family background so as to assist in the moral guidance of each student.

While considerations of hierarchy dictate that students approach their teachers in a respectful manner, it is also true that both teachers and students feel a sense of trust and intimacy with each other. As well as providing individual care for each student in the home room, teachers also stay after school as late as six or seven o'clock to supervise students' extra-curricular activities. When students have personal problems, it is common that they ask their teachers, not their parents, for advice. For example, when a student from junior high school was arrested for shoplifting, the police called his home teacher first, rather then his parents.

A similar teacher-student relationship exists at the university level. In the latter years of tertiary study, when the area of study has been narrowed down, students are divided into small seminar groups. A lecturer is appointed to each seminar group and that lecturer both supervises academic study and acts as a mentor who provides students with moral support.

In response to such close ties, students adopt a subservient role. They have confidence not only in the teacher's ability but also in his or her strength of character.

Coming from such a background, Japanese students may seem to Australian teachers to be rather passive. Many such teachers comment that Japanese students seem to lack initiative, when, in fact, the students are being reserved so as not to intrude into their teachers' teaching space. Equally, Japanese students are deeply disappointed by the business-like attitude of many of their Australian teachers, some of whom are not at all interested in looking after their students. Some comment that Australian teachers lack dignity and tend to be over-sensitive to their students' opinions.

Obviously, teacher-student roles differ greatly between Australia and Japan. In the classroom, it may be useful for the teacher to clarify Australian assumptions about the roles and duties of teacher and learner in order to avoid misunderstanding and unnecessary confrontation.

The Education System

The present Japanese education system is based on what is called the 6-3-3-4 system: six years of primary education followed by three years of early secondary education (middle school), three years of late secondary education (high school) and four years of tertiary education.

Although education is compulsory only for the first nine years, the retention rate at high school level is about 94 per cent. 37 per cent of students go on to tertiary education, which includes universities and two-year junior colleges. In order to enter both high school and university, students must sit for an entrance examination set by the individual institution. These examinations are extremely competitive and the pressure they place on students is often referred to as the 'examination hell'.

As a foreign language, English is compulsory at secondary school level. This means that every child in Japan receives a minimum of three years' English language education. Grammar and reading and writing skills are strongly emphasised, with speaking and listening being relatively neglected.

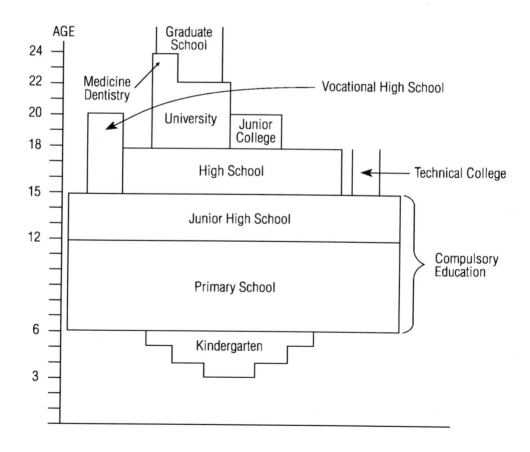

Shinji has been studying in a language school in Perth. His teachers are having a lot of trouble with him and say they find his behaviour overly familiar and therefore offensive.

In fact, Shinji's unreserved behaviour is almost certainly due to his misunderstanding of the roles of teacher and student in Australia. Because the rules governing roles are different, Shinji has concluded that there are none.

What is appropriate student behaviour? How do you expect students to behave towards you?

As a language teacher, how can you explain your expectations to students like Shinji?

Many Japanese students tend to regard activities such as pair and group work, problem-solving and the use of songs and mime in the classroom as playing, that is, not serious learning. Some even find such activities patronising.

Based on your reading and on what you understand of Japanese values and behaviours, why do you think Japanese students might feel this way?

How would you explain your teaching methods to a group of Japanese students who felt like this?

Do you think you should modify your teaching methods to take into account your students' expectations of what should be learned and how?

Why or why not?

Classroom Tasks

■ Task 1 ■

How do Australian English classes differ from Japanese ones?

Divide a large sheet of poster paper into two columns, one headed 'Japan' and the other, 'Australia'.

Under each heading, list the things you did (and do) in an English class.

Here are some questions to get you started:
- ★ How is the furniture arranged?
- ★ Who talks most, the students or the teacher?
- ★ Do the students each have a text book?
- ★ Does the teacher use both English and Japanese or just English?
- ★ What type of exercises do you do?

You go on!

■ Task 2 ■

Do you think it is useful to use Japanese in your English classes?

Draw up a list of the advantages and disadvantages of using it.

Then ask your teacher what she thinks.

Are there any differences in your opinions?

■ Task 3 ■

Are Australian teachers similar or different to Japanese teachers?

Draw up a list of similarities and differences, and use this to explain your comparison to your Australian teacher.

■ Task 4 ■

Below is a list of statements about language learning. In groups, decide if you agree or disagree with them.

1. Speaking fluently is more important than speaking grammatically.
2. Grammer exercises are a waste of time.
3. It is easier to learn a language if the teacher follows a text book.
4. Students learn best if they are having fun, so games and songs are effective ways of teaching and learning language.
5. In learning a language, the teacher is the most important resource.
6. If you can speak a language well, then writing it is easy.
7. A good teacher is one who can explain well.
8. Teachers should not publicly correct their students' spoken errors.
9. The teacher's most important job is to keep quiet and let students talk.
10. The teacher should decide what the student should learn.

■ Task 5 ■

How do you address your Australian teacher?

How do you address teachers in Japan?

How do you feel when you use the Australian system? Explain your feelings to your teacher.

How do you think an Australian would feel using the Japanese system?

CHAPTER ■ NINE

RECOMMENDED READING

General Interest

Christopher, Robert C. 1983. *The Japanese Mind.* Fawcett Columbine Books.

Doi, Takeo. 1981. *Anatomy of Dependence.* Kodansha International.

Friedman, David. 1987. *The Misunderstood Miracle: Industrial Development and Political Change in Japan.* Cornell University Press.

Hall, John W. 1971. *Japan: From Prehistory to Modern Times.* Tuttle.

Kuno, Susumu. 1973. *The Structure of the Japanese Language.* MIT Press.

Mason, R.H.P. 1973. *History of Japan.* Tuttle.

Nakane, Chie. 1984. *Japanese Society.* Tuttle.

Literature

Akutagawa, Ryunosuke. 1981. *Japanese Short Stories.* Tuttle

Ariyoshi, Sawako. 1984. *The Twilight Years.* Kodansha International.

Enchi, Fumiko. 1980. *The Waiting Years.* Kodansha International.

Endo, Shusaku. 1983. *Silence.* Kodansha International.

Kawabata, Yasunari. 1957. *Snow Country.* Tuttle.

Natsume, Soseki. 1969. *Kokoro.* Tuttle.